PRIDE IN THE LION

The History of Newcastle University
Rugby Football Club

Published by Newcastle University Rugby Football Club Vice Presidents' Association
University of Newcastle upon Tyne, Newcastle upon Tyne, NE1 7RU, UK

First published 2007

Design, typesetting and production by Consilience Media, Whitley Bay, Tyne and Wear

ISBN 978-0-7017-0217-5

I would like to dedicate this book to my wife, Pat, who is also a passionate supporter of the Rugby Club, for her help and understanding over many years.

CONTENTS

FOREWORD

A French rugby captain attributed his team's style of play to "une passion pour l'ovale".

Professor Evans has exhibited a similar passion both in his support of the student rugby players of Newcastle University and the daunting tasks of many hours of research required in compiling this history. The serious time spent delving into old papers was certainly rewarded with the pleasure of reminiscing with players of the past thirty years during countless telephone calls and meetings with so many of them.

Tracing the history of the Club through the various colleges, all part of the University of Durham, until the time when the far larger King's College was allowed to stand alone, he has provided the detail that enables the Club, as with any other organisation, to revel in its tradition. A task far more onerous in student clubs with the notoriously poor administration attributed to them.

The student game has always been at the heart of rugby football. Initially, rugby developed in the independent schools, followed by the universities and grammar schools. The university clubs provided an all important facility for players to continue in the game and, in doing so, provided innumerable players, referees and administrators to the growing number of clubs. The spread in the schools sector was followed by growing numbers in the universities.

After some years of decline, the numbers are now growing again and mainly in the student sector with the help of RFU support. Newcastle University Rugby Club is at the forefront in increasing the number of teams playing: more teams in the BUSA competitions, a strong inter-mural league, Freshers' teams and Ladies' teams. Together they make up a thriving club.

The question is often asked, usually in a deprecatory tone, "Why do you play for the University? Why don't you play for a proper club?" Well, the questioner obviously never has. I have been privileged to play in a very good club, in a very successful team and for a number of years. I have many good friends from that team, two thirds of whom had already been students. I presume that I might have had six more seasons there. However, I am very glad that I decided to play with my student peers, fighting for a place, as in any club, playing with a group who by their very nature are more adventurous in extending the boundaries of the game, to say nothing of relating the same to social activities. The innumerable exercises (pranks?) as far as possible conducted within the framework of a 'no damage (lasting) to person or property' policy were audacious and hugely satisfying. As was the sense of 'giving back' something to the Institution of which one was very proud.

I am honoured to have been asked to contribute this Foreword after having spent six years within "that other club". You were always our great rivals albeit we were also King's men – technically that is!

Stewart, the Club and the game are greatly indebted to you. On behalf of all of us a Very Sincere THANK YOU.

W G D Morgan
Hexham, July 2007
Medicals 1955 – 61

PREFACE

There are primarily three reasons for writing this book:

The first is that I believe that student clubs have made, and still continue to make, enormous contributions to the game of rugby football both on and off the pitch but that this is not always fully recognised. I hope that the achievements of Newcastle University RFC over more than a century serve as an example of our importance to the game. This is not solely in developing the skills and potential of elite players, although several of our own players have represented their countries, but in providing opportunities for players at all levels to participate in meaningful, competitive rugby.

The second reason is a desire to share my own feelings of pride in belonging to Newcastle University Rugby Football Club. These have developed progressively since I first became involved with the Club in the 1974/75 season. Since then, I have served in several different academic roles in the University and almost every position that is possible in the Rugby Club – many of them at the same time. However, while I have had many years to develop my knowledge of the Club, most of our players are here for three years only, and their knowledge tends to be limited to that short period of time. They may know little or nothing of the Club's tradition and past achievements and are unaware of the Club's fine record and the challenges that we have faced over more than a century of rugby football. It seems a pity that the young forward who wins, say, the No 8 shirt for the first time may be unaware that internationals John Jeffrey (Scotland) and Ken Goodall (Ireland) once played for us in that position; the stand-off may not realise that Dick Cowman (England) was once our No 10; and the new full-back unaware that he should be in awe of Dave Caplan (England) and Joe Clarkson (USA). Unfortunately, I have discovered from the glazed expressions induced by retelling past deeds that rugby players are not always receptive to history. There is a time and a place for everything and over a pint in the bar after the match or the Club's annual dinner are not the times or places for rugby folklore! Hopefully, this book will provide an opportunity for players and supporters (including and especially parents) to delve into our past at their leisure, remind former players of their own 'glory' years and encourage everyone to uphold our traditions. In saying that, I cannot pretend that more than 30 years' involvement with Newcastle Rugby Club has not been without incident – rugby players are certainly not angels! The contrast between the total commitment on the rugby field with the 'fun' and humour 'on tour' or in the bar, or the lengths to which players may go to attract sponsorship, can be extraordinary. However, it is all part of the enjoyment that has made the 'Newcastle experience' so important in so many people's lives. I have therefore recounted one or two events that might not have everyone's approval but are part of this broader perspective.

The third reason for writing the book is that I became increasingly aware in researching information that it provides an insight, albeit perhaps a small one, into the social development of student life at a provincial university. There has been a gradual transition over the decades from a Club that was almost entirely student run to one that has become almost a 'professional' outfit, with significant staff support – and there is little doubt that we are only part of the way along this particular road! These changes in structure and approach are reflected in the ways that match reports have been written or rugby issues have been debated over the years in Newcastle-based students' magazines, such as *The Northerner*, *Durham University Medical Gazette* and *The Courier*, Durham-based magazines, such as *The New Durham* and *The Palatinate*, and in regional newspapers, especially *The Journal* and *Evening Chronicle*. In order to give a flavour of these changes, and hopefully capture moments from the past, I have quoted extensively from original reports, rather than précis them in my own, duller style. Access to these materials has been possible because of the wisdom of Newcastle University's Robinson Library, Durham University Library and Newcastle City Libraries in archiving copies of student magazines and newspapers. They, together with the nine volume series '*Early History of Northumberland County Football Club*', which is held by the Tyne and Wear Archives Service, have been crucial sources of information – without them much of our rich history would have been lost. However, in consulting these and other sources, I have become increasingly aware of a problem that will face anyone searching for similar kinds of information in the future. In the past, rugby reporting may have been erratic but coverage was broad; nowadays, club rugby, outside the Premiership, is scarcely reported. There was a time when *The Journal* and *Evening Chronicle*, and even the national newspapers, gave very full reports of university matches but, these days, they hardly give us a mention at all. The onus falls on student papers, especially *The Courier*, to preserve details of student rugby for the future. Currently, it gives excellent coverage, including reports of inter-mural matches as well as BUSA fixtures. Long may it continue to do so.

Nevertheless, I am conscious that there will be many errors of fact, and others of omission, in what I have written. I apologise but I have done my best to find accurate information. While researching the past has been a fascinating exercise, it has not always been easy. Sometimes the full information is no longer available, even in the archives, and in other cases it is duplicated but contradictory. Details of the Don's Cup, which was undoubtedly a wonderful competition before it became defunct when Newcastle University was granted its own charter, is just one example of information that has been difficult to find. Reporting, even of the final, has been sporadic and it has often been necessary to infer winners in particular seasons from comments such as "we are determined to retain the Cup again this year" in the build-up to the Cup in following seasons. The problem remains to this day. I have found full details of most matches played against other universities in the past decade or so but, with the exception of fixtures with Durham University, not all of them. Extraordinarily, this even includes some of our matches against Loughborough or Northumbria!

Stewart Evans
Newcastle University, June 2007

Two former club captains, Ed Beckett (left; 2005/06) and Anthony Mellalieu (2006/07), keep a watchful eye on developments from the balcony of the Cochrane Park Pavilion. Club Captain is probably the most demanding position held by a student official, and the Club is greatly indebted to all of those who have acted in this role. Photo courtesy of Tom McNicholas.

ACKNOWLEDGEMENTS

LOTTERY FUNDED

I am most grateful for funding support for this publication from:
- Newcastle University Rugby Football Club Vice-Presidents' Association
- Newcastle University Rugby Football Club
- A grant from the Dove Fund through the former Vice-Chancellor of Newcastle University, Professor Christopher Edwards
- Mr Graeme Kalbraier
- The National Lottery 'Awards for All' programme

My thanks to Jennie Gundill for granting me permission to quote from articles in Newcastle-based student magazines, mostly *The Courier*, Melanie Wood for allowing me to use materials that are archived in the Robinson Library, Paul Robertson (on behalf of ncj Media) for giving permission for me to quote extensively from *The Journal* and *Evening Chronicle*, and John Fletcher for agreeing that I could quote from the Newcastle Falcons website.

Special thanks to Ruth Lunn for proof reading the text and Dan Brady for his advice, skilful design of the book and for organising other aspects of the publication process.

I have received huge help from friends in reporting particular aspects of our history or finding suitable illustrations for it. Professor Tom McNicholas and Jennie Gundill deserve special mention for their help in either taking photographs or helping me to get access to them. In addition, I gratefully acknowledge help in obtaining illustrations or providing information from Glyn Davies, Ed Heggerty, Dave Woodcock, John Bates, John Fenn, Bernard Jones, Mal Stokoe, Ted Wood, John Tarbit, Richard Appleby, John Craven, Joe Clarkson, Simon Best, John Best, John Seymour, Derek Morgan, Danie Serfontein, Stuart Bainbridge, Bess Evans, Tamara Taylor, Ian Cook, Fraser Kennedy, Derek Hawes, Michael Stansfield and Alan Callender and other staff of the Special Collections Room in the Robinson Library.

I am personally disappointed that I cannot remember, or find details of, the various Club Captains (as distinct from 1st XV Captains) who have occupied the post since it was created in the 1980s. They have served the Club magnificently to a person and deserve full acknowledgement for their work. While I have been able to include an 'Honours Board' of 1st XV Captains, I have not attempted to do so for Club Captains because of the patchy information. I hope that they, together with other club officials, will be generous enough to accept blanket thanks for their efforts.

Honours Boards

First XV Captains of Newcastle University RFC

1963/64	Mal Anderson / John Farthing	1985/86	Nigel Grey
1964/65	John Tarbit	1986/87	Chris Jones
1965/66	Robin Poyntz	1987/88	Dave Brown
1966/67	Stu Masheder	1988/89	Nick Johnson
1967/68	Dave Woodcock	1989/90	Graeme Aitchison
1968/69	Bob McManners	1990/91	Tom Seymour
1969/70	Clive Goatman	1991/92	Ali Meadows
1970/71	Chas McGuigan	1992/93	Stuart McGuire
1971/72	John Gibson	1993/94	Dave Rankin
1972/73	Noddy Bateman	1994/95	Nick Thompson
1973/74	Dave Caplan	1995/96	Simon Selkirk
1974/75	Terry McCaw / Roger Rendall	1996/97	Matt Walker
1975/76	Roger Rendall	1997/98	Jimmy Cartmel
1976/77	Dougie Currie	1998/99	Jonny Marston
1977/78	Dave Smith	1999/00	Paddy Seymour
1978/79	Paul O'Donnell	2000/01	Rowan Brown
1979/80	Mike Dudley	2001/02	Walter Scott
1980/81	Robbie Allen	2002/03	Julian Coultas
1981/82	Mark Byers	2003/04	Paul Scott
1982/83	John Hughes	2004/05	Richard Booth
1983/84	Tim Davies / Duncan McDougal	2005/06	Oli Luard
1984/85	Peter Craven	2006/07	Ben Duncan

Internationals

Name	Country
J A S Ritson	England
R G Henderson	Scotland
Brian Keen	England
Ken Goodall	Ireland
Dick Cowman	England
Dave Caplan	England
John Tarbit	East Africa
Sean Avery	Brunei
Joe Clarkson	USA
John Jeffrey	Scotland
Paul O'Donnell	Ireland B
Hugh Parker	Scotland A

Name	Country
Paddy Johns	Ireland
Mike Shelley	England A
Simon Best	Ireland
Rory Best	Ireland
Hugh Vyvyan	England
Hall Charlton	England A
Tom May	England A
Mark Lee	Scotland Sevens
Tim McNulty	Hong Kong
Katie Storie	England
Tamara Taylor	England
Damilola Erinle	England

Trophies

Season	Team (1st XV unless stated)	Competition
1930/31	Armstrong College	Runners-up Northumberland County Challenge Cup
1951/52	King's College	Winners Northumberland County Seven-a-side Competition
1954/55	King's College	Winners Northumberland County Seven-a-side Competition
1955/56	King's College	Runners-up Northumberland County Seven-a-side Competition
1955/56	King's College	Winners Durham County Seven-a-side Competition
1956/57	King's College 3rd XV	Winners Northumberland County Challenge No III Cup
1959/60	King's College	Runners-up Northumberland County Challenge Cup

Season	Team (1st XV unless stated)	Competition
1961/62	Eustace Percy Hall	Winners Northumberland County Challenge No III Cup
1961/62	King's College	Runners-up Northumberland County Seven-a-side Competition
1961/62	Eustace Percy Hall	Runners-up Northumberland County No III Challenge Cup
1964/65	Newcastle University	Winners Northumberland County Challenge Cup
1965/66	Newcastle University	Winners Northumberland County Seven-a-side Competition
1967/68	Newcastle University	Winners Northumberland County Seven-a-side Competition
1968/69	Newcastle University	Runners-up Universities Athletic Union Championship
1968/69	Armstrong College	Winners Northumberland County No III Challenge Cup
1968/69	Henderson Hall	Runners-up Northumberland County No III Challenge Cup
1969/70	Newcastle University	Winners Northumberland County Seven-a-side Competition
1969/70	Henderson Hall	Winners Northumberland County No III Challenge Cup
1969/70	Newcastle University	Joint Winners Universities' Athletic Union Championship
1971/72	Newcastle University Centaurs	Runners-up Northumberland County Senior Shield
1976/77	Newcastle University	Runners-up Universities' Athletic Union Championship
1977/78	Agrics	Runners-up Northumberland County No III Challenge Cup
1981/82	Newcastle University	Runners-up Northumberland County Seven-a-side Competition
1984/85	Newcastle University	Winners of Journal Trophy Division II
1985/86	Newcastle University	Winners Northumberland County Seven-a-side Plate Competition

Season	Team (1st XV unless stated)	Competition
1992/93	Newcastle University 3rd XV	Runners-up Universities' Athletic Union Third Team Championship
1994/95	Newcastle University 3rd XV	Winners Universities' Athletic Union Third Team Championship
1998/99	Newcastle University	Winners BUSA Premier League North A
1998/99	Newcastle University	Runners-up University Championship of England and Wales
1999/2000	Newcastle University	Winners BUSA Premier League North A
1999/2000	Newcastle University	University Champions of England and Wales
2000/01	Newcastle University Women	Winners of the BUSA Northern Premier League B
2001/02	Newcastle University Women	Winners of the BUSA Northern Premier League A
2004/05	Newcastle University Centaurs	Northumberland County Challenge Competition No 4
2004/05	Newcastle University III	Northumberland County Challenge Competition No 5
2005/06	Newcastle University	Winners BUSA Premier League North B
2006/07	Newcastle University 2nd XV	Winners of BUSA Northern Conference 1A
2006/07	Newcastle University 3rd XV	Winners of BUSA Northern Conference 3B
2006/07	Newcastle University 3rd XV	Winners of the BUSA Vase Competition

1

PRIDE IN THE LION

There is no doubt that innumerable players have felt, and still feel, great pride in having played rugby at Newcastle University – pride in the lion, the University's emblem!

What is it that makes Newcastle University Rugby Football Club such a special rugby club? There is certainly no simple answer since different people will almost certainly treasure their association with the Club for different reasons. Nevertheless, there would surely be agreement that we can feel pride in at least the following achievements:

Excellence on and off the field

We have always been renowned as one of the best university clubs in the country based solely on our playing record. Invariably, we are one of the strongest student sides in the country. It is true that we cannot match the successes of one or two of our great rivals in winning trophies but life at Newcastle University provides a wonderful balance between excellence in academic pursuits, personal development and sporting achievement. Sport takes its place, albeit a hugely important one, as part of the academic programme, alongside world quality research, teaching, scholarship and outreach. There should be no conflicts in our aims to provide a student environment based on these goals, even for a young person with aspirations to become a professional rugby player. Rob Andrew, the (then) newly-appointed Director of Rugby at Newcastle Falcons, pointed out in an interview with Luke Edwards, which was reported in *The Courier* in December 1997, that:

"The standard of student rugby in Newcastle is a great encouragement. I hope that, as the universities and Falcons work together, Newcastle will gain a reputation as a place where one can, not only get a good education, but play a high standard of university and club rugby as well."

A decade later we can justly claim that this collaboration has worked – indeed it is, and always was, part of a continuing process. We have always been an excellent nursery for player development. Many of our men and, in recent years, women players have reached the highest levels and several of them have gone on to play international rugby. However, there is much more to the Club than its elite players. Our ethos has always been to provide rugby that will enable individuals to develop their potential at all levels of the game. It is a proud boast of the Club that, in addition to the four men's sides that represent, and bear the name of, Newcastle University in inter-university (BUSA) competitions on Wednesdays, there are another four teams competing in Saturday student leagues, and 12 well-organised teams from various parts of the University playing inter-mural rugby. In addition, two women's teams represent us in BUSA competitions. In other words, week in week out, 22 well-organised teams take the field. The strength of Newcastle University Rugby is still further emphasised when it is realised that our colleagues at Medicals RFC, which is also a University-based club, field a further three or four sides on Saturdays. Durham University RFC and ourselves share the accolade that we field more rugby teams, in other words provide more games of rugby for players, than any other club in the country.

First team rugby of the highest standards. Winning a line-out against Loughborough. Photo courtesy of Tom McNicholas

The spirit of the game

Student rugby is undoubtedly played in the finest traditions of the sport. Literally hundreds of university matches each season, not solely at Newcastle but across the country, are played with huge commitments to the game and passions to winning but within the spirit of fair play.

This does not mean that university matches are soft and un-aggressive. Controlled aggression is very much part of rugby and it is certainly part of the student game. The problem comes when aggression is un-controlled and it escalates into violence – when this happens the beautiful game can become a very ugly one indeed! The Wales – England match at Cardiff in 1980, which was watched by millions on television, was a disgrace, and a complete turn-off as far as recruiting young people to the game was concerned. What sane parents would want their children to take up a sport in which thuggery seemed to be an integral part? In fairness, the rugby authorities are as concerned as anyone in dealing with over-vigorous play and have coped well in dealing with the problem. Although the issue still emerges from time to time, the game generally has a very healthy image for clean and fair play.

However, dealing with issues of over-aggression at a national level is one thing, countering it at club level is another. The position adopted by

Well-organised and well-supported inter-mural rugby.
Cheeky Ladies versus Larrikins. Photo courtesy of The Courier

the Newcastle University Rugby Club's Selection Committee in reacting to the publicity given to this particular Wales – England match was exemplary. Richard Smith recorded it in an article in *The Courier* in February 1980 as follows:

Courier

A stark warning was issued by Mike Dudley, Captain of the 1st XV, on behalf of the Rugby Club's Selection Committee.

Any ungentlemanly conduct or vicious illegal tactics on the rugby field will result in the offenders becoming unavailable for selection.

In the light of the recent disturbing events in the match between England and Wales, where top-level players resorted to brutal and condemnable actions, the University is keen to prevent this from infiltrating the play of our own rugby players.

In an effort to preserve the clean reputation of the Club, any person found guilty of an illegal act, will not be selected for forthcoming matches.

This philosophy has been maintained as part of the Club's ethos, and is reflected in our disciplinary record. Northumberland RFU Disciplinary Committee has kept detailed records for only the past five years. However, during that time, only one Newcastle University player has appeared before it, and he was red-carded for retaliating after severe provocation.

Coping with over a century of changes

Newcastle University Rugby Club has been in existence in various guises for well over 100 years, and has lived through innumerable changes and reorganisations. These have ranged from adjustments in the laws of the game and of the scoring system, especially awards for a try or dropped goal, to changes in the structure of the University (we were once College of Science, then Armstrong College, followed by King's College and finally Newcastle University), to the influx of 'new' universities when polytechnics were granted university charters, to the development of women's rugby, and finally to major changes in the structure of the game itself, including the introduction of national leagues and professional rugby.

Above: Controlled aggression. Rolling forward with secure ball – a strength of many Newcastle teams. Photo courtesy of Tom McNicholas

Below: Durham University have been major rivals ever since Newcastle University was given its own charter and the two institutions separated in 1963. Photo courtesy of Tom McNicholas

Many of these changes have created enormous challenges for the Club but we have survived them all. The demise of student rugby with the advent of national leagues in the late 1980s is a case in point. When the organisation of the leagues became clear, universities were out in the cold. We were not barred from competing in the leagues but would have difficulty in doing so because about a third of the proposed dates for fixtures were in the vacations. It appeared to us that we had been disregarded, in spite of the huge contribution that student rugby had made to the game regionally and nationally. The university clubs had enjoyed superb relationships with clubs in North-east England for decades at junior and senior levels of the game – there can scarcely be a club side in Northumberland, Durham and beyond that has not played against us at one level or another – but suddenly there was a barrier between ourselves and the clubs. We either had to join the leagues, which would give us huge problems in fulfilling fixtures, or lose our contact with the clubs.

After great machinations, we decided that our best course of action would be to join the leagues. We entered them and we believe that we were the only senior university club to do so from the outset – and, despite the problems, we enjoyed the experience. While we struggled to raise teams in vacations, we enjoyed competing with clubs, mostly from Yorkshire, with which we had not previously had fixtures. However, fate (or rank bad planning by the rugby authorities) was against us and we were finally defeated when the World Cup was played in England in 1991. This was because more than half of the league fixtures were scheduled for vacations in that season. Attempting to fulfill them would have been madness, and we were forced to withdraw from the league system. Worse was then to follow because, once out of the leagues, our Saturday team collapsed. Our better players drifted to club sides to play league rugby. However, rather than dwell on our ills, and the total unjustness of them, we joined with our friends from Northumbria and Durham Universities, and persuaded the Rugby Football Union to support a regional system of student leagues, which were to be played on Saturdays – they were an immediate success and remain today, a decade later, a tribute to student rugby.

The Club

There is an enormous difference between a rugby team and a rugby club, although neither term is particularly easy to define. A team is a group of players, often very good ones, who have been brought together with the sole object of winning matches, and better still trophies. A club is much more than this – and Newcastle University RFC is most certainly a club. Friendship, good humour, enjoyment and spirit are essential ingredients. These are qualities in which rugby clubs excel – they are, surely, among the most hospitable gatherings of people in the world (off the field that is!).

A good club spirit also has positive benefits on the field. Players bond and are prepared to give their all for one another. Rituals also become part of the culture, and one of Newcastle University's is a victory song, performed in a huddle which breaks up in a very un-haka-like, twirling 'dance'. Older club members and parents tend to watch its performance with embarrassed, half-smiles on their faces, while locals despair at the way in which 'Newcastle' is mispronounced. Nevertheless, the ritual epitomises much of what is good in the Club – togetherness!

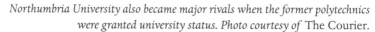

Northumbria University also became major rivals when the former polytechnics were granted university status. Photo courtesy of The Courier.

The first part is sung to the tune of John Brown's body and the second part to a tune that probably has its origins in soccer folklore. The words are:

Forty Geordies went to Rome just to see the Pope,
Forty Geordies went to Rome just to see the Pope,
Forty Geordies went to Rome just to see the Pope,
And this is what they said:

Who's that team we call Newcastle,
Who's that team we all adore.
Well, we play in blue and white,
*And we're ******* dynamite.*
We'll support Newcastle evermore.

We are blue,
We are white,
*We are ******* dynamite,*
Tra-la-la ,tra-la-la, tra la.

The victory ritual. Yet another rendering of "Forty Geordies"!
Photo courtesy of The Courier

2

CLUB SUPPORT

It would be reasonable to expect that such a huge commitment to rugby football at Newcastle University, both on and off the field, would require an equally large investment of administrative staff. Not at all! The spirit and ambience of the Club depend heavily on off-the-field support from a range of different people, who are prepared to give up their free time voluntarily supporting teams vocally from the touchline, providing coaching and training of the highest standards, tendering the injured, fund-raising, organising referees and fixtures, serving behind the bar and a host of other duties. There is a huge 'behind the scenes' effort that goes into each and every game of rugby. Facilities are also important and, again, we are fortunate in that the pavilion at our home ground, Cochrane Park, is one of the best, if not the best, of any university. It overlooks the first team pitch, and this too is as good a playing surface as any in Northumberland. Rugby pitches are also located at the magnificent estate at Close House, which is located at Heddon-on-the-Wall, about 10 miles west of Newcastle.

Student leadership

However, student clubs are unique in the sense that they rely heavily on players in administrative positions and, although we cannot give carte blanche to all of our officials over the years, we have been extraordinarily lucky to have had many outstanding club committees. It follows that we have benefited from innumerable successful dinners, dances and tours. Club officials make mistakes from time to time, mostly attributable to student inexperience, but the huge positives that come from this organisation are the benefits that countless young people gain in developing inter-personal skills, learning to make decisions on which others depend and 'carrying the can', doing so from positions ranging from those of captain, secretary and treasurer to social organiser, website manager and press officer.

Staff support

Staff support is also crucial to the long-term success of the Club because the student body is a transient population – most players are with us for three years only! No sooner has a student learned how to become an efficient secretary or treasurer than he/she graduates and moves on. In a poorly run club, the role is then simply passed on to someone else who learns it all over again starting from scratch. Staff can provide the essential continuity by, for example, providing newly-appointed officials with the information, instructions and contacts that they will need to perform their duties efficiently as soon as they take over.

Director of Rugby John Fenn on the touchline with Graeme Kalbraier, whose son Robbie played in the 1st XV for three seasons between 2004 and 2007. Graeme attended virtually every home and away match during this time – usually travelling from Ipswich by helicopter. He was also a generous benefactor of the Club. Photo courtesy of Tom McNicholas

Several members of staff who have played roles in supporting the Club over the years are mentioned in appropriate parts of the book. In the past they acted in entirely voluntary capacities and this is still largely the case. However, club activities are now coordinated by a Director of Rugby, currently John Fenn, whose part-time post is supported primarily by funds raised by past and present students and the Centre for Physical Recreation and Sport. The Centre also provides excellent support in coordinating inter-mural rugby and the development of women's rugby.

The position of Club President is a significant one, which has been occupied by only three people since Newcastle received its charter in 1963:

- The first President of the Club (as Newcastle University) was Professor M Mac Cooper. He was a remarkable man, whose career has been described beautifully by his son-in-law, John Craven: *Mac Cooper. A Biography* published by Pentland Press in 2000 (ISBN 1 85821 807 1). Mac became Professor of Agriculture at King's College in 1954 and came with excellent rugby credentials, having captained Wellington RFC when they won the New Zealand Club Championship in 1939, winning a blue at Oxford University in his first year there and subsequently becoming captain of that Club. Despite being a New Zealander by birth, he won two caps for Scotland. Due to Professor Cooper's heavy college/university commitments, his involvement with the Club was confined mostly to touchline support and team talks. These have been described as "frightening but at the same time inspirational" by players who attended them. He was awarded a CBE in 1965 in recognition of his services to the agricultural industry.

- Professor Keith Runcorn took over the post on the retirement of Professor Cooper. He was an outstanding, geophysicist, even by world ratings. Peter J Smith wrote of him in the *New Scientist* on 28 April 1983:

    Runcorn has probably made more original contributions to more branches of the subject than any other geophysicist;

but if history judges his work on that basis alone, it will come up with an incomplete assessment. For what would be missing would be the effect of his enthusiasm on others, in ways not recorded in the formal literature...

Who else but Runcorn could give an impromptu hour-long lecture on any geophysical topic and probably have just the right slides in his pocket to support it? For decades yet, whether it be in Newcastle, London, Los Angeles, Sydney or wherever, I expect to see, or hear of, his rising from the audience at the end of someone's lecture with "I just happen to have this slide here which illustrates..."

It was Keith Runcorn's enthusiasm for the game that endeared him to Newcastle University's rugby players, and also his willingness to break off erudite discussions with world class scholars to help over some mundane matter with the Rugby Club. Richard Fielding wrote in the same edition of the *New Scientist*:

*The Rugby-playing 'Prof'. Cartoon of Club President
Keith Runcorn courtesy of the* New Scientist

One of the doughty pack leaders to emerge in the late 1940s from the Manchester scrum of 'palaeo-magnetists' was S Keith Runcorn – a former Cambridge engineer with an almost unhealthy liking for the rough and tumble of the rugby field. Keith Runcorn is now professor of physics, and geophysics supremo, at the University of Newcastle-upon-Tyne – and incidentally the president of the university's rugby club.

- The current President and author of this book is Professor Stewart Evans. He is a marine biologist, who was first appointed to the University in 1970.

Vice-Presidents

Almost all, in fact probably all, former players relish their time at Newcastle, and welcome the chance to keep in touch, not only with their team mates, but the Club as a whole. In the 1980s, a small group of us, in particular Ian Cook (former 1st XV hooker), Dave Woodcock (who captained the 1st XV in 1967/68) and Stewart Evans, organised a Vice-Presidents' Association. It was open to former players, parents and, indeed, all supporters of the Club. One advantage was that it enabled us to 'formalise' links with two people who have given us outstanding support, although neither of them actually played for Newcastle University RFC: W G D (Derek) Morgan and Danie Serfontein. Both of them are Newcastle-trained dentists and, in their playing days (1960s), were stalwarts of the Medicals Club and the (then) parent Durham University RFC. Derek also made his mark as England's No 8. Subsequently, they have continued to make outstanding contributions to rugby football, and each is a Past-President of the Rugby Football Union.

In its heyday, the Vice-Presidents' Association flourished. The magazine *In Touch* was circulated to members and there were two re-unions a season. The Association raised a 'serious' team to play against the 1st XV in an early season fixture. At the end of the season, a social match was arranged between the Vice-Presidents and the 3rd XV. This was followed by the

Above: The South African Prime Minister, Mr F W de Klerk, who engineered the demise of apartheid, with Danie Serfontein, President of the Rugby Football Union, at Twickenham for the England – South Africa match in 1992. This was the first time that the two countries had played at Twickenham since the South Africans had been ostracised from international rugby. Photo courtesy of Danie Serfontein

Left: Founder member and first Chairman of the Vice-Presidents' Association: Ian Cook.

Right: Derek Morgan when he was captain of Durham University in 1958/59

Club's annual dinner – at which the VPs to a man sloughed off the veneers of respectability acquired from their experiences in the world outside to revert to type. Not always a pretty sight but the sound basis of a good time for all!

The Vice-Presidents' XV. This team of former players, shown with Ian Cook (self-acclaimed manager), defeated the University 1st XV in October 1984. Photo courtesy of The Journal

Membership of the Association was always small, reaching perhaps no more than 150 people (certainly hugely short of its potential), and it is now being re-vitalised. The Association has sponsored a Club website (www.nurfc.co.uk), and is planning a range of initiatives for the future.

Touchline support
Of course, support from all quarters is welcome, including parents and casual supporters who enjoy watching fast,

Vice-Presidents' Association magazine

N.U.R.F.C. Vice-Presidents Association

IN T()UCH

Issue no.4 September 1987

open, skilful rugby. A number of the 'fairer' sex usually adorn the touchline, and who better to express their interest than a female correspondent of the *The Courier*. She wrote in January 1969, shortly before the Club appeared in the UAU Final:

Courier

WOMAN'S EYE VIEW

With a team like ours to support, it is more than worth going to watch big inter-varsity matches. The First XV Rugby team on Wednesdays are superb entertainment for the girls (minority that we are!).

Watching 30 (and our 15 in particular) hunky, gorgeous men quickly turn Persil white to chocolate brown as the field turns into a relative quagmire, and...would you believe it?... they can continue to play a first class game of rugby...it certainly adds something to the players' masculinity.

As mud flies on Wednesdays, the games get more juicy (for us standing merely perishing on the brink) and voices near me get shriller. "Come on...". "Oh he's scored again." Blimey that must have been agony." Etc, etc.

They're grand lads – playing or watching (they do get injured etc at times) or touch judging! They need your support... and I can't wait until they win the UAU and my guess is that they will.

Playing to the gallery! Photo courtesy of The Courier

Ciaran McNicholas (No 8 between 2004 and 2007) and two generations of family supporters. Photo courtesy of Tom McNicholas

Newcastle University supporters relaxing at the Dubai Sevens. Photo courtesy of Anthony Mellalieu

Fathers and sons

There is usually a good representation of parents on the touchline, although they show the same pattern of behaviour as their offspring. They are keen supporters for the time that their sons (and nowadays daughters) are here but, with occasional exceptions, then 'disappear' from Cochrane Park. Increasingly, we also have support from inter-generational family groups, in which father and son have both represented the University. The most impressive example is that of the Craven family, in which Newcastle Rugby connections span three generations. John Craven, who had been a captain of King's College RFC, as well as Durham University in 1960/61, married Club President Professor Mac Cooper's daughter. Their son, Peter, followed the family tradition by studying agriculture at the University and captaining the 1st XV in 1984/85. There was one Club dinner, which was attended by all three of them.

Other examples of these family relationships tend to be dominated by prop forwards probably (as they would claim) because they are so fecund. The laws of inheritance seem to decry that props beget props, or at least forwards beget forwards:

- John Seymour, who played as a prop in the 'glory years' in the 1960s, is the father of Tom Seymour (1st XV Captain and flanker in 1990/91) and Paddy Seymour (1st XV Captain and hooker in 1999/2000).

- Andy Keen, son of Newcastle and England international prop Brian Keen, played hooker in Paddy Seymour's team in 1999/2000.
- John Best, who was a prop in the 1970s, is the father of two Irish internationals, prop Simon and hooker Rory Best. John's brother, Garry, was a stalwart of Agrics in the John Jeffrey era.

This previously undiscovered 'Mendelian' law of inheritance can nevertheless be reversed or even broken on some occasions. Alan Hetherington played at stand-off for King's College but his son, Andy, reverted to the front row mould – he was hooker in the early 1990s. Malcolm Martin was a King's College and a County back-row forward in the 1950s, but his son David played at full-back in the mid-1980s.

Peter Craven (carrying the ball), after he had left university and playing for Orrell in a First Division match against Sale in 1987. Peter was University captain in 1984/85. His grandfather, Professor Mac Cooper, had been President of the Club and his father, John Craven, had captained both King's College and Durham University in 1959/60. Photo courtesy of John Craven

The Seymour family: Paddy, John and Tom. John was a 1st XV and County prop in the Club's successful period in the 1960s. Subsequently, his sons Paddy and Tom became captains of the 1st XV

The Best family: Rory, John and Simon. John was loose-head prop in the early 1970s and sons Rory and Simon are current Irish internationals. Simon captained Ireland on a recent tour of Argentina

Outside support

The Rugby Club also receives enormous support from a range of people, both within and outside the University. There are several who will be remembered with great affection by players from the 1970s and 1980s. In particular, Stan Calvert deserves special mention. He was Senior Lecturer in Education and Director of the Centre for Sport and Physical Recreation. His many achievements included election as Chairman of the British Council of Physical Education and Chairman of the Northern Council for Sport and Recreation. However, his interests were broad and he was also a member of the Northumberland National Park and Countryside Committee. Stan was an extremely fair-minded man and a gentleman in the finest traditions of sport. He gave strong support to all sporting activities but undoubtedly retained a special affection for the Rugby Club, and was regularly on the touchline, even in the worst weather. Stan's name is now honoured by a day celebrating sport in which teams at all levels from Newcastle University play all of those from Northumbria University for the 'Stan Calvert Trophy'.

Rod and Steve Fairlea, who looked after our interests on and off the pitch at Cochrane Park for countless years, will also be well-remembered.

At one time, drainage of part of the first team pitch was inadequate and Rod and his staff succeeded in turning a quagmire into a (just) playable pitch for the UAU quarter-final against Bristol in 1977. Steve had the wonderful ability to keep raucous rugby players in order – they simply did as they were told! Similarly, Jackie de Leeuw (now Jackie Seddon) played a priceless role in the Centre for Sport and Physical Recreation office. At one time or another, she must have saved all of the rugby teams from administrative howlers and potential embarrassments in dealings with the outside world.

The Northumberland RFU and, in particular, the Referees' Society, are also bodies that do not always get the full thanks that they deserve. We have always been blessed by an exceptionally high standard of refereeing in Northumberland and often by support that goes well beyond the call of duty. For example, the Society normally supplies qualified touch judges as well as the referee for BUSA matches, and has collaborated with us in training student referees – an initiative that has had a hugely positive impact on the inter-mural rugby programme. And we get the very best officials – Dave Pearson, international and World Cup referee, was in charge of the final of the BUSA Vase when it was held at Cochrane Park in 2007! Alan Christison straddles two camps: he is a former Chairman of the Referees' Society, and remains an enthusiastic Club Vice-President.

Alan Christison: a former Chairman of Northumberland Referees' Society and a Club Vice-President

3

THE AGE OF THE POET
AND THE BIRTH OF
THE DON'S CUP: 1876 – 1914

Finding our roots

Together with our medical colleagues, we were part of Durham University in the latter part of the 19th Century, and for more than half of the 20th Century. The College of Science (situated in the Armstrong Building) and the College of Medicine (then in Northumberland Road) were two prestigious Durham University establishments based in Newcastle. As far as rugby is concerned too, we were part of Durham University RFC. According to an article in the *University of Durham College of Medicine Gazette* (Volume 27, 1926/27, 140-141), the parent Club's records go back to at least 1876.

However, presumably because of the expense and inconvenience of travel for players between Newcastle and Durham, it was difficult for Newcastle-based players to represent the University and two constituent, Newcastle-based clubs were formed: Durham University College of Science RFC and Durham University College of Medicine RFC. These are the roots of the two Newcastle clubs that still exist today. They underwent name changes and survived the 'split' when Newcastle University was granted its own charter in 1963, leading to its independence and separation from Durham University, but both clubs can boast a tradition that is well over a century old. The College of Science RFC has survived three changes in identity:

Late 19th / early 20th Century	Durham University College of Science RFC
1905/06	Armstrong College RFC
1937/38	King's College RFC
1963/64	Newcastle University RFC

The College of Medicine RFC eventually became The Medical Rugby Football Club, known to all and sundry simply as Medicals.

Playing strengths

The College of Science and College of Medicine clubs were both subsidiary to the parent University club and functioned only partly independently. Players were available for selection for the senior Varsity side as a first priority. However, because of the difficulties in travel between Newcastle and Durham, the Varsity team was drawn only from the Durham Colleges in the earliest years. Players from both of the Newcastle clubs were included in the Durham side from 1884 onwards but this started an uneasy relationship that continued until the Durham and Newcastle Universities separated in 1963. Nevertheless, the early Durham University sides were powerful ones. The team was unbeaten in the 1886/87 season, including in its wins the scalps of local senior clubs, such as Hartlepool Rovers, West Hartlepool, North Durham and Westoe. The following season, the Club beat Northumberland County, and in 1888/89 and 1889/90 it was recognised as the strongest club side in Durham County. Several lean years then followed but from 1897/98 there was a resurgence in playing strength and, until the outbreak of the First World War, the Durham University Club continued to perform well against senior clubs in north-east England.

These parts of the University were as familiar to students in the College of Science in the first part of the Twentieth Century as they are to students of today

The front of the Armstrong Building, the oldest building in the University

The arches

The quadrangle and the east side of the Armstrong Building

Records of matches in which the College of Science RFC was involved start from the season 1901–02 when the College's student magazine *The Northerner* was first published. The standard of rugby was certainly lower than that of the parent Durham University Club. Many fixtures were against school sides, including Newcastle Royal Grammar School, Sedbergh School, Durham School and Newcastle Modern School. There is no evidence that fixtures were played against the leading clubs in Northumberland in those days. Part of the reason will have been that fixtures were restricted to Wednesdays, while outside clubs played on Saturdays but, in any case, the likes of Northern, Percy Park, Rockcliff and Tynedale were probably too strong for us. One outstanding player did represent the Club in this era: J A S Ritson was a member of the 1909/10 team (by now Armstrong College). He, as our first international, was awarded caps against Scotland and France in that season. Otherwise, apart from R Steele who was selected to play for Northumberland in 1913/14, there are no records of College of Science players receiving representative honours before the First World War.

We do not appear to have entered the Northumberland County Cup Knock-out Competitions ourselves so that they cannot be used as yardsticks of our performance in these early years. However one of our regular opponents, Newcastle Royal Grammar School (RGS), did so. They won the County Number 3 Cup in 1910/11, and the Number 4 Cup in 1907/08, 1908/1909 and 1911/12. Our results against the RGS suggest that, with the exception of games in the Don's Cup when we were at full strength, we were of a similar standard to the School and it seems likely therefore that our teams were playing at about third or fourth team senior club level.

Most fixtures were probably not taken too seriously, although fitness, especially among the forwards, was evidently seen as a problem. 'Rugby Notes' in the January 1906 edition of *The Northerner* included the comments:

THE NORTHERNER
THE MAGAZINE OF THE DURHAM COLLEGE OF SCIENCE

A word about the forwards. We are a fairly average lot, without any stars, so to speak, but we must work harder. After healing out – and the ball must come out straight at the back of the scrum – the forwards must break quickly and support the three-quarters. This can only be done by a man in good condition; it is therefore the duty of the forwards particularly to keep fit.

The Don's Cup

While the general approach to rugby may have been relaxed in those days, the same cannot be said of the highlight of the season – the match (or matches) against other teams within Durham University RFC, including Durham-based colleges, such as Hatfield Hall and University College, but especially our great rivals, the College of Medicine. The complex history of universities in Durham and Newcastle produced an unparalleled hotbed of intense (but healthy) rivalries. These have continued until today (nowadays Northumbria University is part of the equation) but the rivalry between the College of Science and College of Medicine seems to have been as keen as anything that has followed it. Sir George Hare Phillipson, who was Dean of the College of Medicine from 1892 until his death in 1918, presented a special trophy, the Don's Cup, to be presented to the winners of a knock-out competition between teams within the University. There were no Varsity fixtures on the days of cup-ties so that matches were played by sides that were at full strength.

The importance of these fixtures and the students' approach to them is well-illustrated by a quote from Rugger Notes in *The Northerner* Volume 14, page 91:

THE NORTHERNER
THE MAGAZINE OF THE DURHAM COLLEGE OF SCIENCE

Visions of the coming cup-ties are looming in the Rugger camp, and active preparations to overcome our mortal foes are afoot. Scrum practices, necessary evils now-a-days, are being arranged, and we hope, being carried out in the Riding School, Northumberland Road. This denotes enthusiasm, and such enthusiasm deserves and, indeed, begets success. We are confidently looking forward to the bagging of the Don's Cup, the fight for which is without doubt the great event of our athletic season. Here's to our success!

...When our cup-ties do come round, it is imperative that men turn out and yell for all they are worth. Laboratories and lectures are not excuses and, in fact, we do not see why the College should be open at all on these important days.

Medicals dominated the Don's Cup in the first few years and, indeed, for most seasons before the First World War.

The Don's Cup. *The results of finals up until the start of the First World War. Records of this great competition are patchy and distributed among a range of student publications. Many of the reports that do exist are incomplete. The scores are missing for some years.*

Year	Winner	Runners-up
1901/02	College of Medicine 26	College of Science 0
1902/03	College of Medicine	
1903/04	College of Medicine 14	College of Science 3
1904/05	College of Medicine 20	Hatfield Hall 0
1905/06	Armstrong College 10	College of Medicine 0
1906/07	College of Medicine	
1907/08	College of Medicine 21	Armstrong College 5
1908/09	College of Medicine 30	Armstrong College 8
1909/10	Armstrong College 12	College of Medicine 8
1910/11	Armstrong College 7	College of Medicine 3
1911/12	College of Medicine 14	Armstrong College 8
1912/13	College of Medicine 22	Armstrong College 5
1913/14	College of Medicine	

College of Medicine XV. The photograph is undated but is probably the team that won the Don's Cup (next to the captain) for the first time in 1901/02

The trend was set when College of Science lost to the College of Medicine 0-26 in the first final in 1901/02. The match was held at the College of Medicine's home ground at Heaton; College of Science did not have a ground of their own at that time. The loss was clearly a cruel blow to morale but *The Northerner* reported that a gratifying feature, presumably the only one, was that there were comparatively large numbers of spectators present – 'particularly those of the fair sex'! *The Northerner's* 'tame poet', inspired, according to the magazine, by the near approach of spring but probably more so by disappointment in the performance of fellow students, published the following lament:

THE NORTHERNER
THE MAGAZINE OF THE DURHAM COLLEGE OF SCIENCE

College of Science
Breathing defiance
How did your cup-tie go?
Journey to Heaton
To see the team beaten
By twenty-six points in a row.

College of Science XV in the season 1901/02.
They were runners-up in the final of the Don's Cup

We had to wait until the season 1905/1906 before we eventually won the Don's Cup, now in our new guise of Armstrong College. It was our first piece of silverware. Hatfield College had been dispatched convincingly by 36 – 0 in an earlier match but Medicals were a much tougher proposition. In reading the following account from *The Northerner*, remember that a try was worth only three points in those days, and dribbling the ball was one of the game's recognised and practised skills.

DON'S CUP

ARMSTRONG COLLEGE 10 points
v
MEDICAL COLLEGE 0 points

This match was played at Heaton on Wednesday 28th February. Science had a full team with the exception of Brown for Blizard, the latter being on the injured list. The Medicals started facing a fairly strong wind, Davies taking the kick and Wetherill returning. From some scrambling play, Hood dribbled over the Medical's line, but Cumberledge kicked away before he could touch down. Pearse fielded Chapman's drop-out rather feebly, and a scrum resulted. Wilson followed up a good kick from Turnbull causing Ebb Smith to return weakly to touch. From some loose play Findlay passed to Hearn, who was however tackled before making much ground. A series of scrums followed on the Meds. 25. Lunn made a good run, but the ball was eventually kicked dead. After the kick-out Atkinson was put in possession by Pearse, and ran well, but was pushed into touch. A break-away by Meds. was diverted by Turnbull who kicked dead. Pearse fielded a kick from Seymour, but the Meds. charged down his return and carried play to the Science 25, where Turnbull relieved with a good kick. From play in mid-field Seymour got possession, and after passing three or four men was looking dangerous when he was well brought down by Turnbull. The Science forwards carried the play back to Medics. 25 when the whistle blew for half-time with the score sheet blank.

Science had now to face the wind, and so decided to keep the ball close. After some loose play, in which Smith and Owen were conspicuous, for good dribbles, Wetherill secured and passed out well to Atkinson, who, after making a good deal of ground, was pushed into touch. When in an awkward position, Atkinson made more ground by a good kick to touch.

A series of scrums followed on the Meds. line but, although the Meds had some narrow escapes, no score resulted. The ball was eventually kicked over, and the 25 kick afforded the Meds. some relief. The ☞

☞ Science forwards were now playing a magnificent game and the Meds. could not hold them at all. After some more play in the Meds. 25, Hood secured and dashing through the opposing forwards scored a good try – Owen adding the points.

The kick-off afforded the Meds. only temporary relief as Hearn from a good pass by Lunn made a lot of ground. Bedson and Lunn were playing well together, and were quite as good as the opposing pair.

From a scrum in the Meds. 25, Lunn secured and broke through and scored a good try – Owen again converting.

From the Medical kick-off, Atkinson kicked into touch, and from the line-out Wilson secured and dribbled well carrying the play back to the Meds. 25. Shortly after this the whistle blew for full time.

REMARKS ON THE MATCH
The Armstrong College can congratulate themselves on their fine display against the Medicals, thus causing the Medicals to hand over the cup after they had it in their possession since its inauguration. The principal feature of the match was the brilliant play of the forwards in the second half; they all played with a good even game, and it would be invidious to sort any one out for special mention. Of the halves, Lunn was the best on the field, while Bedson played a good game, his tackling being especially good. The three-quarters all did well to prevent the formidable quartette opposed to them from scoring. Turnbull was very safe at back, his tackling of Seymour when the latter seemed certain to score, eliciting well merited applause.

The victory instilled huge confidence in the Armstrong College team and its supporters, and expectations of great achievements to come. Unfortunately, they were quickly deflated as Medicals soon had their revenge. The following season they regained the Cup. Armstrong had beaten University College in the first round but then lost 0 - 8 to the College of Medicine in the final. *The Northerner* remarked on the splendid nature of the contest and congratulated 'Meds.' warmly on their performance. It was regretted that Armstrong showed 'few of those characteristic wheels and field-long rushes which were witnessed in last year's encounter'.

The Northerner's report of the match was headed as follows:

RUGBY FOOTBALL

"In loving memory of the Don's Cup. Departed this day, Feb 20th, 1907. Greatly regretted."

A more colourful account of the game itself was given by *The Northerner*'s 'tame poet', whose confidence was clearly growing and had now been moved to greater literary heights. It is interesting that, even in those days too, the referee came over as the main culprit for the defeat. An additional point relates to the title of the poem. Rugby was often known simply as 'football' in those days – several well-known rugby clubs, such as Northern Football Club, even excluded 'rugby' from their name.

THE MAGAZINE OF THE DURHAM COLLEGE OF SCIENCE

THE FOOTBALL MATCH

The day was fine as most days go;

Indeed, some say it was more so.

The cold wind blew, the white foam flew,

Our noses were now red, now blue,

Now both at once, 'tis but too true.

"Aha", the captain cries, "oho,

The shine from off the Meds. will go

When our fifteen, both man and lad,

In lightest of light clothing clad,

Make on the field our rushes mad."

The captain's face changed all too soon,

He very shortly changed his tune;

For wild and rapid was the attack,

And heads met earth with many a crack.

Of oaths, strong oaths, there was no lack.

The referee he changed the game,

On him doth rest the heaviest blame.

Had he not been too flush of breath

(And so a critic to me saith)

The Meds. would soon have met their

death.

And now the tables quickly turned,

And now hot anger in them burned.

Our foes soon bravely scored a "try",

Determined now to do or die.

Then scored a goal right rapidly.

And now a man is wounded seen,

Stretched out upon the muddy green.

Like hero in the Trojan war,

Although his wound has strick'n him

sore,

He takes his place – game as of yore.

The watchers cry now "Coals", now

"Sines,"

In deep bass voice or feeble whines.

The time draws nearer to the end.

Oh! that mistakes they could amend,

Or Heav'n some marvel now would send.

So keen did one supporter grow -

And him by sight you all must know -

He stood apart, as in a dream,

His mouth wide fixed, his eyes did gleam

For naught save this, our valiant team.

But no! relentless time goes on,

The days of miracles are gone

No valiant man the Cup can save,

All hopes are lying in the grave;

The loss is great. Toll for the brave!

It was not until the seasons 1909/10 and 1910/11 that Armstrong College won the Cup again. *The Northerner*'s report for the first of these seasons emphasised the strength of our forwards:

DON'S CUP FINAL

ARMSTRONG COLLEGE 12 points v MEDICAL COLLEGE 6 points

Several hundred spectators assembled at Heaton to witness this match – one of the most important in the North. Science supporters, judging from their cheering, were superior in force to the supporters of our opponents. It was a pleasing sight to see so many ladies present – doubtless it was to obtain grace from the fair that strengthened the chivalrous hearts of our men.

Of course, our chances of winning had been discussed many days before the day of combat. Our worthy captain was praying for rain months ago in order that our staunch forwards might have the opportunity of showing their ability. The Medicals three-quarter line looked very formidable on paper: Averall, Humphries, Chapman and Sutcliffe formed this. We were all quite alarmed, yet pleased for the 'Varsity sake, to read in the account of the international match at Twickenham on Saturday that Chapman was decidedly the best of the English three-quarters! However, we have three-quarters as well, and we have forwards! We congratulate J A S Ritson on being "capped" for England against France. He was the mainstay of our "pack", and was always in the thick of things. It was curious to notice how often these two internationals, Chapman and Ritson, rolled together in the dust during the match. Surely they have not old scores to wipe off!

In the end, the victory was ours. Imagine if you will, every Science student making a mighty explosion in the Chem Lab. – you then have some idea of the applause at the close of the game – for the Don's Cup was ours, is ours, and, we hope, ever shall be ours. Thus ended one of the most cleanly and keenly contested games ever played at Heaton. In conclusion, we offer our heartiest congratulations to the team who have brought honour to the College by their achievement. May they live to fight as well another Cup-tie. To the Medicals – consolation! Let them try all their patent medicines to their team to give them strength to endure their defeat.

The triumph in the following year gave our poet the opportunity to demonstrate his talents still further. This time it was one of our three-quarters who won the day. We do not know the name of the player who performed so stunningly but he was clearly a very exceptional person!

THE MAGAZINE OF THE DURHAM COLLEGE OF SCIENCE

THE RUN OF OUR CRACK THREE-QUARTER

Here he comes sparkling,
(How the crowd mark him!);
No smoking nor froth,
Nor tumult nor wrath,
But cheery and speedy
He hastens along, conflicting, strong,
Fit for the scrum and the run.
Rising and leaping,
And leaping and dashing,
Rushing and sweeping,
Thrusting and smashing,
Swinging and flinging,
Bounding and springing,
Twining and twisting
Around and around;
Collecting, accepting
The ball's quick rebound;
Now smiting and fighting,
In turmoil delighting,
Confounding, astounding,
Dazzling and startling the eyes all
around.
Fleeting and speeding,
And shocking and rocking,
And rattling and battling,
And running and stunning,
And hurrying and scurrying,
And working and jerking,
And heaving and cleaving
A way through the throng.
Not falling and brawling and sprawling,

Nor fumbling and stumbling and
tumbling,
But driving and riving and striving;
Now grounding then bounding and
rounding.
And dribbling and troubling and
doubling;
Feinting and fending and wending,
Punting and lunging and plunging,
Clattering and battering and shattering.
And rushing and flushing and brushing
and gushing,
And flapping and rapping and clapping
and slapping,
And curling and whirling and purling
and twirling,
Advancing and prancing and glancing
and dancing,
And thumping and flumping and
bumping and jumping,
And dashing and flashing and flashing
and crashing;
And so ne'er retreating, but always
advancing,
Opponents still meeting and always
defeating
(Sounds and sights such as this are
worth seeing),
All at once and all o'er, with mighty
uproar –
And this way our three-quarter did score.

33

While the College of Medicine was usually dominant in these early years of the Don's Cup, they were almost invariably opposed by the College of Science / Armstrong College in the final. With the exception of the losing appearance of Hatfield Hall in 1904/05, teams from Durham colleges were generally out-classed in the early years of the competition. It is presumably for this reason that they combined together to field a Durham Colleges team in 1910/1911. This Colleges team was to become a major strength at times in the future but, at first, they fared no better than the individual colleges had done before them. In their first outing in the Cup, the team was beaten 44 – 0 by Armstrong College.

The outbreak of war witnessed an almost complete cessation of University Rugby. Armstrong and the College of Medicine pooled their resources, due to the shortage of players, turning out as Newcastle Colleges. Even then, they had difficulties in raising a side. *The Northerner* reports that they beat Sunderland 21 – 8 with a team of only 12 men, and were also three men short in a 6 – 0 victory over the Royal Grammar School in the 1914/1915 season.

OF BLACKGUARDS, SWINE AND BLEATING SCHOOLGIRLS: 1919 – 1939

Medical glory

A new set of conditions prevailed after the Armistice of the First World War. Large numbers of Newcastle-based students, many of them returning from the war, wanted to play rugby and, in order to accommodate them, a new system was devised within Durham University RFC. Previously, the Medical College and Armstrong College clubs had played only on Wednesdays but now both were permitted to function as senior clubs, playing games against leading club sides on Saturdays. Medical and Armstrong players would still be eligible to represent the Varsity side but Durham University RFC fixtures would be midweek and limited to some dozen or so matches a season. It must have seemed the ideal solution to the Newcastle clubs, and playing results justified the development. Teams were strengthened by returning ex-servicemen and there was a huge improvement in playing standards compared with pre-war days. Student rugby had arrived as a force in Northumberland and has remained strong ever since.

Both the College of Medicine and Armstrong participated in the Northumberland and Durham Senior Clubs' League, which involved all of the region's strongest clubs. There were 19 of them in 1920/21 although, as the game developed popularity and new clubs formed, the number of competing teams had increased to 39 by 1938/39. Positions in the table were based on percentage of matches won with other clubs in the league. Not all clubs had equally strong fixture lists but nevertheless the league tables gave at least an indication of relative strengths of clubs in the region.

Both Medicine and Armstrong competed successfully in this company. However, it was the College of Medicine club that led the way. Their playing record between 1919/20 and 1924/25 was nothing short of magnificent. They won almost three-quarters of their league matches, finishing between third and seventh in the final Northumberland and Durham Senior Clubs' League tables.

The performances of Armstrong College and the College of Medicine in the Northumberland and Durham Senior Clubs' League from 1920/21 – 1938/39. There is no information for 1933/34. The two clubs combined together in 1932/33 to play as Combined Colleges, and Medicals ceased to play as a separate club for the next five seasons. However, Armstrong College contributed to the Combined Colleges team for only one season.

Season	Number of clubs competing in League	Armstrong/ King's College		College of Medicine/ Medicals	
		Percent wins	Position in League	Percent wins	Position in League
1920/21	19	40	14	73	5
1921/22	19	33	16	75	3
1922/23	21	67	9	69	7
1923/24	24	37	16	50	13
1924/25	24	23	22	39	15
1925/26	23	20	21	33	18
1926/27	23	4	23	21	22
1927/28	23	13	23	23	20

1928/29	28	32	21	23	25
1929/30	29	45	16	32	23
1930/31	31	31	23	31	24
1931/32	27	55	11	10	26
1932/33	26	-	-	-	-
1933/34	No info				
1934/35	26	64	8	-	-
1935/36	29	40	17	-	-
1936/37	29	25	24	-	-
1937/38	30	15	29	25	23
1938/39	39	47	18	73	4

More impressively still the College of Medicine competed in four of the first five finals of the Northumberland Challenge Cup that followed the War. They were victorious in two of them.

1920/21	Percy Park 10	College of Medicine 8
1921/22	College of Medicine 30	Northern 0
1922/23	College of Medicine 12	Northern 3
1924/25	Seghill 9	College of Medicine 0

Medicals also monopolised the Don's Cup, winning it for six successive seasons after the War.

The Don's Cup. The results of finals between the First and Second World Wars.
Records of this great competition are patchy and distributed among a range of student publications. Information for some seasons is missing.

Year	Winner	Runners-up
1918/19	College of Medicine	
1919/20	College of Medicine	
1920/21	College of Medicine 34	Armstrong College 0
1921/22	College of Medicine	
1922/23	College of Medicine 8	Armstrong College 0
1923/24	College of Medicine 9	Armstrong College 0

1924/25	Armstrong College	Durham Colleges
1925/26	Durham Colleges	Armstrong College
1926/27	Armstrong College 11	Durham Colleges 0
1927/28		
1928/29		
1929/30	Durham Colleges	Armstrong College
1930/31	Armstrong College 8	College of Medicine 0
1931/32	Durham Colleges	Armstrong College
1932/33	Armstrong College 12	College of Medicine 3
1933/34	Armstrong College	College of Medicine
1934/35	Armstrong College 23	College of Medicine 0
1935/36		
1936/37	Durham Colleges 9	College of Medicine 3
1937/38	King's College 6	Durham Colleges 5
1938/39	Medicals 22	Durham Colleges 9

Not surprisingly, many Medicals were capped by Northumberland. They dominated the county scene for several years after the War. There were no less that six of them in the team selected to play Cheshire in 1920/21, and for this and the next three seasons many county teams included four or five Medicals.

*Above: The crest, which still adorns
the balcony of Cochrane Park's
pavilion, is that of Armstrong College
– a fine reminder of our past!*

*Left: The pavilion at Cochrane
Park has been the Club's 'home'
since the First World War*

Armstrong College RFC: another force to be reckoned with

While Armstrong College was over-shadowed by the College of Medicine's playing record immediately after the War, the Club was also making its mark. It now had its home ground at Cochrane Park, and although the playing surface needed improvement, this was a major step forward. It is also gratifying to know that, during this period, it supported the achievements of its great rivals. A paragraph in the book produced in celebration of 100 years of Medicals Rugby (*The Medical Rugby Football Club 1898-1998*) suggests that an excellent relationship existed between the two student clubs. It refers to the 1924/25 County final in which the College of Medicine lost to Seghill, reading as follows:

> The College XV were well supported in this final with most of the staff and students attending, as well as many students from Armstrong College who all supported the team in a very sportsman-like manner.

Not that things were always sweetness and light! An account in *The Northerner* of pre-match 'negotiations' before the final of the Don's Cup in 1922/23, which the College of Medicine won 8-0, is less kindly:

THE NORTHERNER
THE MAGAZINE OF THE DURHAM COLLEGE OF SCIENCE

To write an account of such a game as the Don's Cup Final this year is by no means easy. But before attempting to do so a few words on the 'Sportsmanlike' behaviour of our opponents, the Medicals, might not be out of place. To refuse to play on our ground, because it was in too bad condition, but to quite willingly play on their own ground, rather savours of the 'Post-War Sportsman' so often depicted in Punch. This for two reasons: firstly, because as everyone knows, a team always plays better on its own ground than its opponents; and secondly because the Medicals knew that the uneven condition of the surface would be very detrimental to their superior backs.

Probably the finest season that Armstrong experienced after the War was in 1922/23. Most detailed club records have been lost in the passage of time but *The Northerner* published full details of 1st, 2nd and 3rd XV results in that season, presumably because they were so good.

THE NORTHERNER
THE MAGAZINE OF THE DURHAM COLLEGE OF SCIENCE

1st XV
Played 18; won 12; lost 6

Oct 14	Hartlepool O.B.	Won	34-3
Oct 21	Old Novos	Won	11-3
Oct 28	Northern	Won	11-10
Nov 4	Gateshead Fell	Won	11-3
Nov 11	Percy Park	Won	21-5
Nov 15	Bede College	Won	22-3
Nov 18	Tynedale	Lost	5-19
Nov 23	Durham School	Won	16-8
Nov 25	Gosforth	Lost	8-13
Dec 6	Medicals	Lost	3-43
Dec 9	Darlington	Won	11-8
Dec 16	South Shields YMCA	Lost	0-8
Jan 13	Gosforth	Won	16-8
Jan 20	Tynedale	Lost	0-6
Feb 3	Gateshead Fell	Won	6-3
Feb 10	Tynedale	Won	15-5
Feb 14	Medicals (Don's Cup)	Lost	0-8
Mar 3	Hartlepool OB	Won	23-9

NORTHUMBERLAND SENIOR CUP

Mar 10	Percy Park	Lost	3-11

2nd XV
Played 18; won 10; drawn 1; lost 7

Oct 21	Old Novos II	Won	10-0
Oct 25	Durham Colleges	Won	15-3
Oct 28	Northern II	Won	16-0
Nov 4	Gateshead Fell II	Won	14-0
Nov 11	Percy Park II	Won	30-0
Nov 18	Tynedale II	Lost	0-15
Nov 21	Royal Grammar School	Won	48-0
Nov 25	Gosforth II	Lost	6-10
Dec 9	Winlaton Vulcans II	Won	5-0
Dec 13	Medicals II	Lost	9-18
Jan 13	Gosforth II	Lost	0-13
Jan 20	Tynedale II	Lost	0-26
Jan 27	Percy Park II	Won	42-0
Jan 31	Durham Colleges	Won	5-3

☞

Feb 7	Medicals II	Lost	0-8
Feb 10	Durham City II	Lost	0-8
Feb 17	Old Novos II	Won	6-0
Mar 3	South Shields YMCA	Drawn	3-3
	NORTHUMBERLAND SENIOR SHIELD		
Mar 10	Medicals II	Lost	0-14

3rd XV

Played 12; won 3; drawn 2; lost 7

Oct 21	Sunderland III	Lost	0-26
Nov 4	Blyth II	Won	9-3
Nov 18	Durham City III	Won	14-5
Nov 25	Gosforth III	Lost	10-12
Dec 9	Westoe III	Lost	5-13
Jan 20	Durham City III	Lost	0-21
Jan 27	South Shields YMCA III	Lost	3-9
Feb 10	Sunderland III	Won	6-0
Feb 17	Percy Park III	Lost	0-3
Feb 24	Blyth II	Drawn	3-3
Mar 3	Medicals III	Drawn	3-3
	NORTHUMBERLAND JUNIOR CUP		
Mar 10	Tynedale III	Lost	0-16

There are several interesting features of these results. Even though Armstrong were strong, the College of Medicine's dominance is all too evident. With the exception of the draw achieved by Armstrong's 3rd XV all fixtures against Medicine were lost. Nevertheless, the Armstrong Club clearly had strength in depth. They were holding their own against the best Northumberland clubs, including Gosforth, Northern, Percy Park and Tynedale, not solely at first team level but at second and third team levels as well.

Nevertheless, Armstrong boasted only one Northumberland County player in this heady period, R G Henderson. He was also capped by Scotland in 1920/21.

Declining standards

Regrettably, the success of the Newcastle student clubs was not to last. Playing standards of the College of Medicine, in particular, declined dramatically. The position of Medicals in Northumberland and Durham

Senior Clubs' League dropped so that, from the mid-1920s onward, they were close to the bottom of the table and few matches were won. What is more, they lost their hold on the Don's Cup and there were no more appearances in the Northumberland Challenge Cup Final for another 20 or so years. Poor attitudes of incoming students were blamed but there were also problems faced by fourth and fifth year students who were expected to attend lectures and clinics on Wednesday afternoons, and were therefore unable to attend training on those days.

Armstrong College's playing record during this period of decline was scarcely better than that of the College of Medicine. However, while the Medicals' performance was now uniformly poor, Armstrong had mixed fortunes. The Club was actually bottom of the Northumberland and Durham Senior Clubs' League in two successive seasons 1926/27 and 1927/28 but won more than half of its fixtures in the 1931/32 season, finishing in 11th position out of 27 clubs.

Armstrong's finest achievement during this period was in reaching the final of the County Challenge Cup in 1930/31 season. The team lost

The Armstrong College team (or at least most of them) for 1929/30

to Northern but after an excellent game. *The Journal*'s correspondent described it as follows:

The Journal

NORTHERN'S TENTH CUP FINAL SUCCESS
Why College Lost
SPLENDID GAME ON HEAVY GROUND
Northern 11; Armstrong College 3.

Northern appearing in their 20th Northumberland Senior Cup-final, defeated Armstrong College, who have never before played at this stage, by a goal and two tries to a try, at the County Ground, Gosforth, on Saturday, and so won the trophy for the 10th time, their last success being in 1926. The ground had been partly cleared of snow, but there was a covering in both '25s'. Naturally, the pitch was heavy at the start and ploughed up by the end of the game.

Northern won because they snapped up their chances in the first half, when mishandling by the College players gave openings to the winners. A try in the first few minutes of the game came as a nasty shock to Armstrong, and gave Northern confidence. The winners did not show any superiority over the College except that on the whole they had the more frequent possession in the scrums, while they made headway in the loose mauls through weight.

On a day when handling was at a discount the College attempted this more often than Northern, who preferred the short punt and follow-up, and scored two tries in this way. On the other hand when Armstrong tried the same tactics things did not come off for them, and Gillespie, the Northern full back, fielding the ball capitally and kicking well to touch, was always a force to be reckoned with when it came to kicking in the open. Whitley and Hodgson were also prominent in this way.

HODGSON OUTSTANDING
It was a dour game forward, each side putting in some fine work, but the other outstanding individual was undoubtedly Hodgson. Thornton, Gallacher, Morpeth and Croft were also prominent Northern forwards. Whitley played a sound game, his kicking to touch being of much advantage, while he also handled safely. Of the other Northern backs, Criddle and Peebles formed the better wing, and the latter ▶

44

▶ proving a rare opportunist.

On the College side Morgan did not have a good day, though he was plucky in stemming forward rushes. Bowerbanks and Gibson were the most conspicuous in the College 'threes' and Goldson, although well marked, played a sound game at scrum-half. McComb was uncertain in handling a difficult ball and Ellis, on the other side, was the surer. Among the College forwards Piercey, Irving and Connor, together with McPherson, put in some capital loose work and hard tackling.

The first score came when Morgan dropped the ball at his feet from a kick by Criddle about 30 yards from the line. Peebles got up to kick ahead, and, although hard pressed, managed to control the ball and score. The College rallied, but Northern came back again, and from a punt by Hodgson, which the College defence failed to clear, the Northern forwards took the ball through and Croft dribbled over for a second try, which Hodgson converted. Northern had to touch down several times after this, and when they set-up a counterattack the Armstrong line had a narrow escape. From a cross-kick the defence was at fault, and Peebles, who had crossed, dribbled over; but a five-yard scrum was ordered. In a fine rally by College Simpson unluckily dropped a pass when positioned to beat Peebles for the corner of the flag.

THE BEST TRY

During the second half the game was chiefly forward. Armstrong soon took play to the Northern line and Gibson scored in the corner. Faulty handling spoilt other College attacks, and when they tried to kick and follow-up they found Gillespie safe. Northern came back into prominence in the last ten minutes of the game, when they scored their best try. Whitley started the movement from a scrum, and after passing along the line Peebles crossed just as he was tackled. The Armstrong defence was at fault in not tackling Criddle in the first place.

The game was much more interesting than some finals seen at the County Ground, and a large crowd had plenty to enthuse over. Mr J H Eddison ably refereed. The cup was presented to G Morpeth by the Northumberland RU president, Mr A Emerson.

Reorganisation

Despite our relative independence during this period, we were still part of Durham University RFC, and the parent club became concerned about the generally poor performances of the two Newcastle teams in the late 1920s and early 1930s. It resulted in a major reorganisation for the season

1932/33. It was agreed that Armstrong and Medicine would no longer play Saturday fixtures. Instead, their players, together with those from Durham Colleges, would be included in two teams that would represent Durham University. One side, which would be known as Durham University, would select the best players from Durham Colleges, Armstrong College and the College of Medicine. The other team, which would be known as Combined Colleges, would be based in Newcastle and would be composed of the best of what was left of Armstrong and Medicine.

While the Armstrong College Club was clearly apprehensive, it was prepared to do its best to make this scheme work successfully. The Rugby notes in *The Northerner*, Volume 32, Number 3 included the following advice:

THE MAGAZINE OF THE DURHAM COLLEGE OF SCIENCE

With reference to next year's arrangement I would like to say that, unless there is complete cooperation, the scheme will fall flat. We have had little or no encouragement from any other club and therefore it is up to members of Armstrong College RFC to show that they are capable of running a thing as a success.

...The whole scheme, if successful, will give Durham Varsity a much higher standing in the rugby world and other Varsities will learn we hope to respect the palatinate jerseys.

As it turned out, the scheme was a disaster. It did not succeed in changing playing standards beyond an initial, short-lived improvement. The Durham University side did well for the first couple of seasons of the new scheme but its performance deteriorated progressively thereafter. It won few of its matches in 1936/37, finishing 25th out of 29 clubs in the Northumberland and Durham Senior Clubs' League – one place below Armstrong College (who had by then withdrawn from the scheme and reverted to playing Saturday fixtures in their own right!). The Combined Colleges team performed abysmally from the outset. It was bottom of the Northumberland and Durham Senior Clubs' League, with an 8% record in its first season (1932/33). At the end of the 1933/34 season, Armstrong withdrew from the agreement and the Combined Colleges team, which still had the support of Medicals, was re-named the Varsity 'A' XV. This failed to bring about any change in its fortunes.

Despite earlier statements of support, blame for the failure was heaped firmly on the shoulders of players from Medicine and Armstrong, at least by the Honorary Secretary of Durham University RFC. His forthright notes on 'University Rugger' published in the *University of Durham College of Medicine Gazette*, Volume 34 included the following comments:

> At the end of the season, when it was decided to give the present system another year's trial, certain promises were made by the Varsity Committee... but although we kept our part of the bargain certain playing members did not keep theirs... hardly had the season started before a few dissatisfied unsporting blackguards from both the College of Medicine and Armstrong College commenced to raise trouble. Notices were posted, little meetings were held and gradually the above-mentioned gentlemen persuaded a few more weak-willed souls to join their ranks. It was pointed out to one or two of the ringleaders that this was hardly playing the game, and quite definitely not giving the Combined Colleges a sporting chance. How can a side hope to win matches if several members go on to the field expressing their strong dislike of the side they are playing for? I am glad to say that several men appreciated our point of view and dropped their propaganda, but there still a few swine who keep up the badly-used attitude and go bleating about College and Union like so many schoolgirls. Let us have none of it.

Another attempt at reorganisation

The formation of King's College in 1937, which resulted in the amalgamation of academic activities in Armstrong College and the College of Medicine, prompted another attempt to bring the two rugby clubs together this time as a single team representing King's College. According to the student publication Union Sauce (which seems to have survived between 1936 and 1938 only) Armstrong were in favour of it, but Medicals were not. There were signs of a recovery in playing strength of Medicals and by now they too had withdrawn support for the Durham University 'Combined Colleges' Saturday team. Once again they were competing in the Northumberland and Durham Senior Clubs' League in their own rights – and were doing well!

They did not combine so that two clubs remained at Newcastle after 1937: King's College RFC and the College of Medicine RFC (which decided to rename itself Medicals). Whether or not any of these developments heightened rivalry between the constituent clubs within Durham University is unclear. However, the Don's Cup was still a fiercely contested competition – never more so than in the season 1937/38! That season appears to typify the intense commitment that had not changed since the Cup was first introduced at the beginning of the Century.

The rules of the Don's Cup were probably modified in different years. It appears that usually, but certainly not always (especially in the very early years), there were only three teams competing (Medicals, King's and Durham Colleges). The normal programme was for two of the clubs to play one another in the first round, and then for the winners to play the third team in the final. However, in 1937/38, each club played both of the others in a league in the preliminary part of the competition. There was no clear outcome from the series of low scoring matches, each club winning once and losing once:

Medicals 7, King's College 3
Durham Colleges 4, Medicals 0
King's College 11, Durham Colleges 5

There was then a play-off between King's College and Medicals for a right to play in the final. Low scores continued but King's reversed the result of the first contest, winning 3 – 0.

The final was therefore played between King's College and Durham Colleges at Durham. King's won 6 – 5.

It was Medicals' turn to win the Cup in 1938/39. They now had a strong team and were fourth in Northumberland and Durham Senior Clubs' League – easily their best performance since the early 1920s. The Second World War then intervened but the post-war period was to see another period of boom for the rejuvenated Medicals Club.

5

Of Medicals and the King's Men: 1946 – 1963

History repeats itself

The extraordinary success of the Medicals (then College of Medicine) after the First World War was repeated immediately after the Second World War. Once again the return of older, stronger and more experienced ex-service men was the telling factor. This time the effect lasted for slightly longer. The period of success after the First World War had covered six successive seasons from 1919 until 1925, compared with eight seasons from 1947 until 1955 in the second post-war period.

Information is patchy but Medicals was successful by any measure one cares to take:

- There was no longer a Northumberland and Durham Senior Clubs' League but final playing records for senior clubs in Northumberland are available in *The Early History of Northumberland Football Club* for the first five seasons post-war. Medicals had the best playing record of all clubs in 1946/47 and played consistently well in the other seasons of that period. The Club continued to hold its own in this heady company not only for these five seasons but until the mid-1950s.

Comparison of the playing records and relative rankings of 14 Northumberland Rugby Senior Clubs for seasons immediately after the Second World War.

Club	Season				
	1945/46	1946/47	1947/48	1948/49	1949/50
	Percentage matches won				
Ashington	52	53	72	70	56
Coll. of Commerce	41	55	24	36	24
Gosforth	24	26	39	60	35
King's College	**50**	**20**	**71**	**25**	**71**
Medicals	53	82	60	58	70
Northern	67	72	63	54	49
North Shields	73	63	52	61	48
Old Novos	22	28	40	45	41
Percy Park	79	78	75	86	83
Rockcliff	7	31	57	47	41
Seghill	72	64	64	31	50
Swan Hunters	50	57	70	29	35
Tynedale	59	79	69	67	61
Wallsend	39	21	43	11	42
Positions based on percentages					
Ashington	7	9	2	2	5
Coll. of Commerce	10	8	14	11	14
Gosforth	12	12	13	5	12=
King's College	**8=**	**14**	**3**	**13**	**2**
Medicals	6	1	8	6	3
Northern	4	4	7	7	7
North Shields	2	6	10	4	8
Old Novos	13	11	12	9	10=
Percy Park	1	3	1	1	1
Rockcliff	14	10	9	8	10=
Seghill	3	5	6	10	6
Swan Hunters	8=	7	4	12	12=
Tynedale	5	2	5	3	4
Wallsend	11	13	11	14	9

- The Don's Cup was dominated until the early 1950s.

The Don's Cup. The results of finals after the Second World War.
Records are patchy and distributed among a range of student publications. Many of the reports that do exist are incomplete.

Year	Winner	Runners-up
1943/44	Medicals	
1944/45	Medicals	
1945/46	Medicals	
1946/47	*Final between Medicals and Durham Colleges but no record found of the result.*	
1947/48	Durham Colleges	Armstrong College
1948/49	Medicals	
1949/50	Draw: Medicals 6; King's College 6*	
1950/51	Medicals 3	King's College 0
1951/52	King's College 9	Medicals 8
1952/53	Durham Colleges 14	King's College 8
1953/54	King's College 5	Medicals 3
1954/55	*No records found*	
1955/56	Draw: King's College 3; Durham Colleges 3	
1956/57	King's College	Medicals
1957/58	Kings College 14	Medicals 0
1958/59	Durham Colleges 16	Kings College 3
1959/60	King's College 14	Medicals 6
1960/61	Durham Colleges 17	Medicals 5
1961/62	Durham Colleges 22	Medicals 5
1962/63	*No records found*	

* King's College wrote to Medicals after the final asking for a date for a play-off but did not receive a reply.

- Records of the composition of the Durham University 1st XV are sparse but, for one available in 1944/45, there were 12 representatives from Medicals.
- The Club finished as runners-up in the Annual Northumberland 7-a-

side tournaments in 1949/50 and 1950/51, losing to Northern on both occasions.

- Exceptional numbers of Medicals were awarded Northumberland County caps in the post-war era. In the 1951/52 season, county sides against first Cumberland and Westmorland, and then Yorkshire, included no fewer than five Medics.

The average numbers of Northumberland county caps awarded to members of King's College and Medicals clubs per county match. This is based on team sheets included in The Early History of Northumberland County Football Club. *Averages are shown rather than total numbers of caps because a few team sheets are not available.*

Season	King's College	Medicals	Season	King's College	Medicals
1946/47	0	0.4	1955/56	0.6	1.3
1947/48	0.2	1.6	1956/57	2.0	0.9
1948/49	0.2	3.3	1957/58	0	1.0
1949/50	0.8	2.0	1958/59	0	1.0
1950/51	0.5	2.0	1959/60	2.6	0.9
1951/52	0	3.8	1960/61	3.3	1.0
1952/53	0.4	3.6	1961/62	0.6	0
1953/54	0.8	3.2	1962/63	1.2	0
1954/55	0.7	2.2			

However, it is in the Northumberland Challenge Cup Competition that Medicals excelled. They were, for a time, the outstanding club in Northumberland at a time when their major rivals, Northern and Percy Park Club, were nationally strong, including several international players in their ranks. Medicals appeared in five cup finals during this period, winning two of them. Their record speaks for itself:

1946/47	Percy Park 13	Medicals 0
1947/48	Percy Park 10	Medicals 3
1951/52	Medicals 5	Northern 3
1952/53	Medicals 14	Percy Park 0
1953/54	Percy Park 6	Medicals 0

To cap it all, Medicals were also innovative. Although it is unlikely that they are the only ones, they can claim to have invented 'lifting' in the lineout. A report in *'The Early History of Northumberland Football Club'* suggests that even greater heights could be achieved with some imagination and a team of circus acrobats:

> WHY NOT ARRANGE A LINE OUT VERTICALLY? Most players will have seen or heard of the acrobatic feats of one, W I Hay (Medicals) who is hoisted above by his fellow men in a line out by a smaller colleague gaining regular possession of the ball.
>
> A writer who claims no copyright, having "no objection to being regarded as an amiable lunatic", wishes to delve further into this matter. He queries: is the lifter guilty of obstruction in so far as he is preventing an opponent tackling the man who has the ball? On the other hand, should an opponent tackle the lifter, would he incur a penalty by tackling a person not in possession of the ball?
>
> Possibly the answer is that nothing in the laws prevents either team having 14 men in the line out arranged vertically, rather than horizontally, and the ball propelled into the field of play to a great height by the 15th – probably the scrum half, he being the smallest.

As had happened after the First World War, Medicals' success was not sustained. One outstanding player, W G D (Derek) Morgan, who gained international honours while still at university, gave substance to the pack but it is evident from match reports that the 1st XV was becoming progressively less strong. Playing records gradually deteriorated, including a humiliating defeat by Gosforth 70 – 0 in October 1961. Regrettably Derek Morgan was injured in this match, and was forced to leave the field of play with head and knee injuries at half-time and another player, Danny Rowlands, joined him on the side-lines during the second half. This was at a time when replacements were not allowed – a problem that was to plague Newcastle University in a Universities' Athletic Union final a few years later. However, while these misfortunes put the Gosforth – Medicals result into a different perspective, they are precisely the kind of luck that seems to beset a team that is down on its fortunes. It was bad luck that was to remain with the Medicals Club for several years.

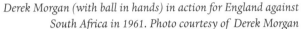

Derek Morgan (with ball in hands) in action for England against South Africa in 1961. Photo courtesy of Derek Morgan

King's College: another force to be reckoned with

The performances of King's College teams in seasons immediately after the war was erratic but the Club was still very strong. Playing records were the third and second best respectively in the county in the seasons 1947/48 and 1949/50 (see above). However, as Medicals' dominance tended to decline from the early to mid-1950s, King's remained strong. They more than held their own in fixtures with leading clubs. Defeats were taken seriously. So much so that the Editorial comment of the *King's Courier* on 10th February 1956 read as follows:

EDITORIAL

We have to print a sad item of news concerning the King's versus Northern Rugby game. We do so with regret. It was the Rugby Club's second defeat of the season, and their first defeat by a club in the North-East; their other loss was to Leeds University.

It is with deep regret we announce that

KING'S COLLEGE RUGBY FOOTBALL CLUB

lost 9 pts. to 6 pts. to

NORTHERN

28th January, 1956

No flowers (only Bass) by request.
Will their friends accept this
(the only) intimation

King's College also lost to Northern in 1960/61 and this time cartoonist Dudley Hallwood was present, recording lessons learned from the defeat for posterity.

Dudley Hallwood's version of the King's College – Northern match in 1961.
From the original cartoon presented to John Tarbit

Some of the Club's notable post-war achievements include:

- Winners of the Northumberland County 7-a-side Competitions in 1951/52 and 1954/55. King's also reached the final of the competition in 1955/56 and 1961/62, losing to Northern on both occasions. They reached the semi-final of the competition in 1956/57.
- Winners of the Durham County 7-a-side Competition in 1955/56 beating Billingham 8 – 0 in the final.
- From the early 1950s onwards, King's College and, to a lesser extent Durham Colleges, began to monopolise the Don's Cup (see above).
- Good numbers of players were awarded Northumberland county caps, especially in the seasons 1956/57, 1959/60 and 1960/61.
- King's College (and Durham Colleges) now became the main sources of players for Durham University 1st XV.

The composition of Durham University 1st XVs in post-war years as shown from occasional team lists included in **The Early History of Northumberland Football Club**

Season	Players selected from:			Percent King's College players
	King's College	Medicals	Durham Colleges	
1944/45	3	12	0	20
1952/53	3	9	3	20
1953/54	3	8	4	20
1954/55	5	2	8	33
1955/56	4	5	6	27
1956/57	9	4	2	60
1959/60	7	2	6	47
1961/62	6	1	8	40
1962/63	9	0	6	60

- King's reached the semi-finals of the Northumberland County Challenge Cup in 1955/56, losing to Gosforth.

- The 3rd XV were winners of the final of the County Challenge Third
  Team competition in 1956/57, beating Gosforth III 8 – 6, and Eustace
  Percy Hall 1st XV (a newly-formed King's College club which had
  now taken over the role of King's College 3rd XV) were runners-up to
  Northern in the Junior Cup competition in 1961/62.

*Action in the Don's Cup First Round in 1959/1960: King's College versus Durham
Colleges. John Craven, King's College captain, threatens the line. King's went on
to beat Medicals in the final of that season. Photo courtesy of John Craven*

Runners-up in the County Challenge Cup in 1959/1960

Perhaps the most notable achievement of King's College was in the Northumberland Challenge Cup Competition. The final in 1959/60 was lost to Gosforth. The Club can claimed to have 'kick started' Gosforth for this was the beginning of an incredible period in which that Club won 22 out of 26 successive County finals.

Unfortunately, the final was a one-sided affair. John Pargeter reported in *The Journal*:

THE JOURNAL

RESULT WAS NEVER IN DOUBT

Gosforth win
in a canter

Gosforth won the Northumberland Rugby Cup by the biggest margin for 23 years when they defeated King's College 22 – 6 in the final on the County Ground on Saturday.

The result, however, occasioned no surprise. It was expected, even I fancy by King's, which explains why the game was disappointingly lacking in "bite".

At no time was there any doubt about who would win, even when King's led 3 – 0 at half-time. Significantly, too, all the College points came from penalty kicks, whereas Gosforth scored six tries.

Gosforth were infinitely superior behind the scrum. King's positional alignment was beyond comprehension and it was most extraordinary why G Blackett at fly-half did not go through the gaps left so invitingly. He limited himself however with handing-on the ball and it was left to R W Hoult to carve the openings. The most vivid memories will be the tries themselves, especially the four scored by wing three-quarters. J Coker gave one of his finest displays, and his tremendously powerful bursts down the left wing to score three tries were without a doubt the highlights.

King's must have planned to deprive Gosforth of the ball, but they failed. In the line-out D Campbell and G N Smith were supreme. The scrummage figures were interesting. In the first half, each pack won seven scrums but two of Gosforth's were against the head. In the second, King's won 13 out of 18 scrums, winning 3, and losing one, against the head.

Dudley Hallwood also attended this match, giving his own interpretation of events. He describes the craggy forwards in King's pack, which was particularly strong at this time. It included Brian Stoneman who subsequently played in England trials and was unlucky not to follow Derek Morgan as England's No 8.

Dudley Hallwood's cartoon of the Northumberland
Senior Final: King's College versus Gosforth

Above: King's College team in 1959/60, captained by John Craven
Below: The Durham University team, which won the UAU Championship in 1950/51

What of Durham University RFC?

As might be expected with such strong playing strengths in the Newcastle teams, the parent club Durham University was also strong. The Club reached finals of three Universities' Athletic Union (UAU) competitions, winning the trophy in 1951/52 when it beat Bristol, sharing it after a draw with Swansea in 1954/55 but losing the final, 3 – 6, to Loughborough in 1956/57. During this post-war era, the Club also provided Durham County with 17 players.

Despite these successes there had been disquiet within the parent Club since the end of the Second World War about the lack of coordination between the Newcastle- and Durham-based players. An article in the Durham-based magazine, the *Palatinate* on 25 February 1949 included the following comment:

Palatinate

The Varsity XV lost to Leeds 9 – 14 at Durham. The low standard of the Durham side, which included 6 county men, was due to the lack of team spirit and common aim which always exists when Newcastle and Durham attempt to combine.

Blame was apportioned squarely on Newcastle in 1954/55 when Danie Serfontein (who was subsequently President of the Rugby Football Union) was Captain. The *Palatinate* commented on 3 December 1954:

Palatinate

Surely the time has come for more coordination in sport between the Durham and Newcastle divisions of the University. The successful University Rugby XV, which defeated Manchester University by 11 points to 5 on 24th November, was selected in Newcastle and no invitation was sent to the Durham selectors.

The team, supposedly representative of the whole University, was posted in King's College Union, four days before Serfontein, the University Captain, phoned it through to the Secretary at Durham. One Durham player was dropped despite the brilliant Rugby which he has been playing.

Then, the team from the first UAU match was selected on the bus coming back from Manchester. Two Durham members were present but not the official representatives and, once again, players of repute were left out.

Ironically, this was a year in which Durham won the UAU!

Nevertheless, similar sentiments were being expressed in Newcastle. A 5 – 13 loss at the hands of Hull University in 1959/60 resulted in the following comments in the report of the match in the *King's Courier*:

KING'S COURIER
Durham University Rugger
NEED FOR REGULAR VARSITY SIDE

The disadvantages of drawing the occasional university side from three clubs, Durham Colleges, Medicals and King's, were amply demonstrated in the UAU championships match against Hull at Heaton Road, last Wednesday.

Though weakened by the absence of W G D Morgan and M Hymas, Durham showed evidence of individual ability, yet lacked the team spirit and cohesion of the Hull side, who have the advantage of playing regular fixtures as a set university team.

There was contrast between the disjointed efforts of Durham and the smoother, more penetrating team work of the Hull side ...

There was a similar feeling in the next season, after a defeat by Leeds University:

... This playing together was emphasized just last Wednesday when Durham University with a mixed team from the constituent colleges were given a lesson in team work by Leeds University. That Leeds University play together regularly was obvious.

What of the future?

The relationships between the parent club and its constituent clubs came to a head when it became clear that Newcastle University was to be given its own charter. A new university, Newcastle University, which would be based on King's College (and would therefore include the Medical School), was to become independent of Durham University.

The split eventually occurred on 1 August 1963. However, planning the future of sports clubs began in earnest a couple of years beforehand. The issue was: should King's and Medicals combine to form a single team representing the University or should they retain their original identities and continue as separate clubs? Many Medicals preferred the latter, which was understandable in many ways. The Club had a long tradition as one of the foremost clubs in North-east England and therefore had much to lose if it was simply absorbed into the grander scheme of things.

The debate that followed in the *King's Courier* was mature and well-informed. Extensive quotes are given from three articles that appeared in November 1961, not only setting out the case but recommending the ways in which rugby should function in the new set-up. In each case, the articles argue for achieving excellence, rather than in promoting narrow self interests. The articles themselves were written by the Sports Editor of the *King's Courier* (hopefully an independent observer), Dennis Bratton, the captain of King's College RFC, and Derek Morgan, the best known and most respected player representing Medicals.

The editorial comment is an obvious attempt to knock a few stubborn heads together:

KING'S COURIER
SPORTS EDITORIAL

... The main problem, and perhaps one of the most weighty problems in College sport at the moment, is the division between King's and Medics. If this situation is allowed to continue then the new University of Newcastle is bound to suffer. It is essential that Newcastle University should come into existence in fine style and thus build up a tradition that it will sorely need.

Granted that Medics have a fine record and one which they naturally wanted to keep, but they must realise, and King's too, that the new University must come first. Make no mistake about the influence that sport has – it brings a school, college or University to the notice of every place in which they play. Look at the fine example the Combined XI football team are ▶

▶ setting. Only last Saturday they hammered Nottingham University 8-1 in a superb effort. They are helping to bring Newcastle to the fore. Let's have a rugby team that does the same.

The effort must be made NOW – on the eve of the separation – so that when the new University does come into existence we can give it a good send off. So come, Medics and King's, let's have your views on how rugby in Newcastle should go. Do you want a team that can do justice to the new University, a team whose loyalties are not divided, a team that will be a TEAM?

F.S.

Derek Morgan argued as follows:

KING'S COURIER

RIFT IN RUGBY

Will Medics go it alone?

The name of Durham University stands highly not only amongst other universities but also in the larger sphere of club rugby in those areas. Bedfordshire, Cornwall and Ireland, where the University Club has earned the respect of opponent and spectator alike. Unfortunately, the Rugger Club – as also is the case with other sports – suffers from many miles of Great North Road separating the two main constituent communities, King's College and Medics, and Durham Colleges.

The basis for success in any team game is "team work". This important factor only becomes part of one's armament when the team has the opportunities and facilities for training and playing together regularly. This is borne out when it is realised that the better teams produced by the University have been those in which one of the Constituencies has provided an exceptionally large proportion of the members – as did Medics in the early 1950s and King's in the mid-1950s; periods when the UAU Championship was won or narrowly lost on a number of occasions.

Four years ago an attempt was made to extend the fixture list of the University Club from the miserable half dozen matches usually played. Percy Park, Gosforth, two of the leading clubs in the North East, and a County Selectors' XV, were played ▶

66

▶ without loss. These matches were of great help to the team in its bid to win the Championship which it narrowly failed to do, losing 6 - 3 to Loughborough in the Final. The constituent clubs however expressed their dislike for Saturday University fixtures and the venture was regrettably dropped.

With the advent of the new University of Newcastle the problem appears to have solved itself!

The Durham Colleges will naturally assume the title and obligations of the University of Durham. Doubtless hard fought battles with Newcastle will be a highlight of the programmes for both clubs... Newcastle however, still has the division of Medicals, founder members of the present University, and King's. King's Rugger Club want the co-operation of Medicals in forming a University Club, running a number of sides with regular fixtures, in an effort to bring Newcastle rapidly to the top.

It is doubtful however whether Medicals wish to participate. They wish to retain the autonomy of the present club while retaining the right of members to play for the University whose matches would be mid-week only. Tradition plays a large part in this attitude for the club is without doubt more famous than its King's counterparts, and although it is in a lowly position and likely to remain so for a while the record of past achievements is an impressive one. A sense of "betterness" and being apart from King's also complicates matters, a large majority being in favour (regrettably) of a complete separation from the rest of King's, with the development of their own social amenities, paralleling the position of the London Hospitals.

...a compromise aimed at preserving "Medicals" yet retaining their right to play for the University seems to be the solution. The University putting out two teams, Medicals lowering their ranks a little, and the remainder to adapt themselves to a suitable level of club rugby in the area supplemented with inter-college and inter-faculty matches.

The University team – the important factor – together with the second XV – would require a ground of the highest standard complete with full amenities including a flood lighting system at least of sufficiently high standard for training; a facility enjoyed by all the major clubs in the area.

The final requirement for success is – STAFF SUPPORT.

Dennis Bratton also identifies several of the components of a successful Newcastle University Club in his vision of the future:

KING'S COURIER

VARSITY RUGBY FUTURE

In the near future King's College and the Medical School will combine to form the University of Newcastle and Rugby as one of the major sports can make a great contribution in establishing the name of the new University in its formative years. With the change in status, both King's and Medicals Rugger Clubs should combine to form a single University Club as other Sports Clubs are already doing for it is as a University Club that the future of rugger inevitably lies, and not as separate clubs. To field a University side composed of players from only one of the clubs would be ridiculous and not truly representative of the best fifteen available. First allegiance of all players, and that matter all students, should be to the University.

King's are almost unanimously in favour of a single club whilst it seems that Medicals have some doubts and are afraid that their identity will be lost on integration with the larger club. The last thing wanted is for Medicals to lose their name as they have a great tradition behind them, being one of the oldest clubs in the North of England. Let me hasten to add, however, that it would be very selfish and not in the best interests of the University if they did "go it alone".

The first essential is a University XV playing regularly and composed of the best fifteen players available in the club. To provide a good reserve strength and provide a stepping stone to the full University side, a second XV on the lines of Oxford Greyhounds should be created of present King's and Medicals 1st XV standard. Below this in the club structure there could be two teams of equal playing standards, Medicals A XV and University A XV, playing with 2nd XV fixtures.

To cater for all the people who want to play rugby without going down to University 10th XV the founding of residential hall and faculty sides is much more desirable. This season two teams were started at Eustace Percy Hall and the experiment has proved highly successful with both teams playing local 3rd and 4th XV club sides. It is hoped that this system of hall rugby will spread to other residential halls.

Medicals could keep their identity as a club within a ▶

club in this system with two teams, together with Medicals A XV, to form a unit equivalent to a residential hall.

Prestige from beating the other universities is great and if Newcastle University could become UAU champions in the first few years then this would be a great step forward in putting the University's name on the map. The playing strength is there and if all players and parties concerned enter into the new venture wholeheartedly and united, Newcastle University would become the strongest rugby club in the North East and able to take on the might of any provincial University in the country.

D R BRATTON

Reaching a compromise

The Early History of Northumberland Football Club includes a report dated 16th October 1963 which stated that the plans for the new Newcastle University Rugby Football Club were now complete. It was a complex compromise of the kind in which universities specialise:

The Newcastle University 1st XV would draw from the best available players from King's and Medicals, and would represent the University in the UAU Championship. This team would play on Wednesdays and Saturdays, taking over the best of King's and Medicals fixtures and representing the University at senior club level.

The former King's College 1st XV, without the players selected by the new University 1st XV, would become the Newcastle University 2nd XV. It would be known as Centaurs. Implicitly it would not include Medicals.

Medicals would continue to run four sides. The first team would play at senior club 2nd XV level (ie be on a par with Centaurs).

In addition, constituent clubs sides (nowadays referred to as inter-mural sides), including Eustace Percy Hall, Henderson Hall, Armstrong College and the Agricultural Society would play on both Wednesdays and Saturdays. They would play against one another and other student sides on Wednesdays, and against the 3rd and 4th XVs of club sides on Saturdays.

Thus an uneasy truce had been agreed but at least a structure had been created. Some features were to prove strengths in future years, others were to be weaknesses. However, a new and exciting era had begun for Newcastle University RFC.

The Irish international Paddy Johns, who studied dentistry at Newcastle, and was a major force in the pack in the late 1980s. He went on to win a total of 40 caps for Ireland. Photo courtesy of Inpho Photography

An assessment

There is little doubt that the strength of Newcastle University 1st XV was enhanced by this arrangement. Outstanding Medical players now joined former rivals from the rest of the University and the team flourished, doing outstandingly well for the first seasons of its existence. Although standards have fluctuated over the years, the Club has always benefited from the inclusion of Medics, two of whom, Dave Caplan in the 1970s (England) and Paddy Johns in the 1980s (Ireland), have been of international standard.

Regrettably playing standards at Medicals declined. This had been implicit in the reorganisation but, despite it, the Club's 1st XV continued to play Saturday fixtures against some senior clubs in the mid-1960s. The results were poor. Consequently, the quality of fixtures decreased but the results failed to improve and the Club was in crisis. An Extraordinary General Meeting was held in June 1964 and it did prove to be a very extraordinary meeting. According to the Club's history (*The Medical Rugby Football Club 1898 – 1998*), it was proposed, and subsequently passed, that the Club should open its membership to postgraduate Medics and Dentists. Whether or not the rules were subsequently broadened still further is unclear. In practice the Club has become an open one. Since 1964, non-Medical students and even some players from outside the University (who are not Medics) have played, and still do play, for the Club.

However, despite its problems and the controversial nature of the Club's reorganisation, several positives have emerged. Except in the minds of some older Medics, the rivalry with the rest of the University has gone for ever – it died in 1963! Nevertheless, Medicals has regained its stature as a fine rugby club, and has maintained much of its pride and famous tradition – helped undoubtedly by continuing to play at its home ground in Heaton. It has made, and continues to make, major contributions to the game of rugby football as a whole:

- The Club runs three of four XVs on Saturdays, including a 1st XV which competes in the Durham and Northumberland League (Division 2 or 3), and a Freshers' team that competes in the North-east of England Students' League. A Wednesday side also competes in the University Inter-mural League. In other words, each week Medicals provide rugby for some 60 or more players.

- The Club performed outstandingly in winning the national Pilkington Shield in 1995/96, beating the Cornish Club Helston 16 – 6 in the Final.

- Remarkably, and probably uniquely, Medicals have provided two Presidents of the Rugby Football Union: D W G (Derek) Morgan and Danie Serfontein. Their contributions to the international, national, regional and local (Newcastle University and Medicals) development of rugby, at student and senior levels, have been immense. That one is "as Welsh as the proverbial leek" (*The Courier*, 1961) and that the other has a clear Springbok accent simply adds to the intrigue.

GLORY YEARS: 1963 – 1970

The Rugby Club's record in its first seven seasons was remarkable. An excellent summary of the successes in this period was given in an article, published in *The Courier* on 10th March 1970, the day on which the 1st XV was due to meet Bangor University College in the final of the Universities' Athletic Union (UAU) Championship:

Courier

To make two appearances in the final of the Universities' championship in two years is a measure of how strong university Rugby has become in the seven years since the foundation of King's College as a university in its own right...

Since 1963 the strength of the side has improved tremendously. The results against former partners and now keen rivals have got better and better. The club has produced two internationals, Brian Keen for England and Ken Goodall (rated the best No.8 in the world) for Ireland; and numerous county and UAU players. In pot hunting expeditions, the Northumberland Senior and seven-a-side cups have rested in our trophy cupboard. ▶

> ▶   Both of the touring South African University sides, Pretoria and Orange Free State, played the university two years ago and the first fifteen themselves have toured extensively.
>
> As the club goes from strength to strength we can only hope that the Freshers each year will be of the standard necessary for these successes to continue.

It should be added that the correspondent was unaware, at the time of writing, that Dick Cowman would go on to play at stand-off for England, and that the County Sevens' trophy would be won for a third time at the end of the 1969/70 season.

Descriptions of the first of the UAU finals, against our rivals Durham University, and the matches against South African universities are given chapters (7 and 15) in their own right. However, as *The Courier*'s article stressed, this was a time of many fine achievements.

In the beginning

The very first match for the newly-formed Newcastle University RFC was against Percy Park on 20th October 1963. It was at their Preston Road Ground in North Shields. Bearing in mind students' reputation for fast, expansive rugby, it was extraordinary that the University's first score was a pushover try! This is how it was reported in *The Courier*:

Courier

Encouraging Newcastle Win

KEEP THIS UP!

Solid game by forwards

Percy Park 3, Newcastle University 11

For their first ever fixture Newcastle University were without their captain Mal Anderson (injured) and forward Sid Gale (County trial) and so fielded a pack with only two forwards having previous university rugby experience. ▶

▶ In the first fifteen minutes Percy Park, playing with the wind, attempted three long penalty kicks, the last of which dramatically hit the upright. The University then began to play more as a team. After some solid tackling by the centres, the back row managed to drive the ball down to the Percy Park line. S Bott was then able to cross the line only to have the try disallowed. However, in the ensuing scrum the University pack with a strong shove wheeled the Percy Park forwards and with a tremendous forward surge pushed over the line for the University's first try.

Whether or not a pushover try is the most satisfactory way for a new university team to score its first points is debatable.

The University pack then began to take charge of the game and, with H Fletcher jumping high in the lines-out and the rest of the forwards rucking well, the Percy Park pack were driven back five or ten yards from bunches on the university line.

The second half opened with the University pack forcing their way deep into the Percy Park half and, by securing a large amount of the ball from the set scrums and lines-out, they stayed their for long periods. They were supported by some lengthy kicking by the inside backs.

The second University try came from a long and penetrating break by Higgins, who, although half tackled, recovered enough to pass to G Jackson. The winger took the ball well and ran hard to score in the corner. J Farthing converted from the touchline.

With the University now well on top, the pack nearly pushed the opposing forwards over the line. However, they heeled the ball and scrum-half Askham put Higgins over for the last try. The University played open Rugby for the last 15 minutes but failed to score again.

Percy Park kicked a consolation penalty goal.

This was a promising start to the season by the University, the pack in particular exceeding all expectations.

The Club had a strong record in Saturday club matches throughout this period, performing well against most of the leading clubs in the area. With the exception of the Gosforth club, which was becoming one of the most powerful sides in the country, each of them was defeated at least once between 1963 and 1970, and overall far more games were won than were lost. Even Gosforth was severely tested in games with us.

The results of Saturday club games between 1963 and 1970. Wins are highlighted in blue; losses in red. Details from *The Journal*.

	1963/64	1964/65	1965/66	1966/67	1967/68	1968/69	1969/70
Alnwick						8 – 6	3 – 3
Billingham	15 – 9	8 – 6	9 – 0	27 – 0	24 – 8		
Blaydon	9 – 17	19 – 0	3 – 9	19 – 0	8 – 3		0 – 3
Carlisle						24 – 11	14 – 9
Durham City		11 – 5		8 – 11			14 – 3
Egremont							11 – 3
Gateshead Fell	9 – 3		6 – 9		17 – 3	8 – 0	
Gosforth	6 – 14	6 – 13				13 – 14	
Harrogate			0 – 5	20 – 14			
Middlesbrough	3 – 10				0 – 9		14 – 11
Morpeth	21 – 3	6 – 13					14 – 3
Newcastle City Col.		25 – 3	34 – 0				
North Durham					3 – 6	11 – 3	
Northern				14 – 3	6 – 14		6 – 6
Old Novos	19 – 3	42 – 0	9 – 15	3 – 3			
Percy Park		13 – 6	19 – 0	8 – 5		14 – 11	6 – 12
Rockcliff	8 – 3	5 – 9		23 – 3			
Stockton			0 – 3	0 – 0	19 – 6	13 – 6	
Sunderland	6 – 3	6 – 5	14 – 0	5 – 11	8 – 16	13 – 11	17 – 8
Tynedale		8 – 0	6 – 8	19 – 3			
West Hartlepool	24 – 0	6 – 14	8 – 11	0 – 11	8 – 12	8 – 6	19 – 0
Westoe		12 – 6	23 – 0	3 – 3	23 – 5		32 – 3
Whitehaven	13 – 5	8 – 5		6 – 14	11 – 19		15 – 20

Northumberland County champions: 1964/65

The team's finest hour in club rugby was to come in the 1964/65 season when, under Captain John Tarbit's leadership, the 1st XV became Northumberland County champions.

Newcastle University's record leading up to the final was impressive:

First round: Medicals were dispatched 21 – 0.

Second round: there was a 14 – 6 victory over Morpeth. This was an excellent win over a good Morpeth side. The first paragraph of the report in *The Courier* revealed a growing tide of new-found optimism:

Courier

QUARTER-FINAL PLACE AFTER FINE WIN AT MORPETH

Morpeth O.E. 6pts; University 1st XV 10pts

It's a year for t'cup lads. At last a measure of spirit was instilled into the team to bolster the unarguable talent. The pack started at a tremendous pace, knocking the Morpeth team – who have an excellent record this season – right out of their stride, and they were fit enough to maintain their early momentum.

Quarter-final: the team overcame Newcastle City Colleges convincingly 33 – 5.

Semi-final. Naturally, things became harder as the possibility of reaching the final loomed closer. The semi-final against Percy Park, which was played on our opponents' ground in North Shields was a particularly severe test. *The Courier* summed up the situation as follows:

Courier

Percy Park crumble to University's 1st half onslaught in cup semi-final

COUNTY CUP AHOY FOR RUGBY?

Roper, Henry & Dunn tries represent all-round show by Tarbit's men

NORTHUMBERLAND COUNTY CUP – Semi-final
Percy Park...6 1st XV...9

On Saturday, the University 1st XV beat Percy Park R.F.C. by three tries to a try and a dropped goal and now play either Gosforth or Rockcliff in the final of the Northumberland Senior Cup. The final will be played at the County Ground, Gosforth on April 10th. This is the first time the University has reached the final since 1960 when as King's College they lost to Gosforth by 22 points to 6.

The Final: Terry Muir's report in *The Courier* published on 5th May 1965 says it all:

Courier

Varsity Rugby Champions!

Tarbit's supermen run Rockcliff off feet with display of skill and fitness

NORTHUMBERLAND R.U. SENIOR CUP FINAL
Newcastle Univ. 12 pts., Rockcliff 3pts.

The University put the right finishing touch to a splendid season when they came out worthy winners of the Northumberland Senior Cup on April 10, beating Rockcliff by 12 pts to 3 at the County Ground, Gosforth.

Rockcliff started as favourites since they had already beaten the Varsity in an earlier club game and had been able to play together right up to the final whereas the middle of the Easter vacation was not the best of times for the University.

This latter disadvantage was partly offset when the whole University ▶

▶ team assembled in Newcastle from all over the country four days before the match. These days were spent in training and discussing tactics and must have been a deciding factor for in the match itself the University showed themselves a fitter and more balanced side.

Kicking off with the wind Newcastle went straight into the attack and after ten minutes the ball was held in a tight scrum and a defender caught offside. Brittle kicked the easy penalty. But now it was Rockcliff's turn to attack. They tried several three-quarter movements and, despite some hard tackling by the Varsity, managed to score a try in the corner. It was unconverted.

The University forwards fought well against a heavier but less mobile pack and worked well together. J Tarbit and A Smith were prominent in the loose. Back row forwards, S Masheder and D Arnold, were also outstanding, managing to subdue County fly-half, Kyle, and thereby restricting the scope of Rockcliff's three-quarters.

Ten minutes before half-time, the University prop, Keen, dropped a goal from in front of the posts. There was no further score in that half and the Varsity turned to face the wind with only a three-point lead. However, it was only minutes after half-time that Rockcliff were penalized and Brittle kicked his second penalty goal. Rockcliff's confidence was now upset, while the Varsity handled and ran with more assurance.

Some good work by J Barlow brought play to near the Rockcliff line. The ball was won from a tight scrum. Full-back, I Hind, joined in the three-quarter movement, providing the overlap for C Henry to score in the corner. The Varsity were now well in command and finished the match in attacking vein.

John Tarbit's team that won the Northumberland Senior Cup in 1964/65.
Photo courtesy of John Tarbit

Dudley Hallwood's cartoon of the Northumberland Senior Cup Final courtesy of The Journal.

The Club also had strength in depth, illustrated by the success of the Second XV, Centaurs, reaching the semi-final of the Number 2 Cup. They lost narrowly, 3 – 5, to Gosforth.

Next: University champions

The Club's first season in the Universities' Athletic Union (UAU) Competition was not successful, although a dismal performance against Hull University produced what must be the shortest match report ever. The complete version in *The Courier* was:

Courier

Hull University 0 pts.
Newcastle University 0pts.

Some Rugby matches are immediately forgettable – this was one of them.

Nevertheless, much greater things were to follow. The first UAU Final reached by Newcastle University was against Durham in the season 1968/69. Although we lost that final under desperately unfortunate circumstances (Chapter 7), it was necessary to wait for only another year for the Club to reach the Final for the second time. On this occasion, it was against University College, Bangor. The result was a draw with the two clubs agreeing to share the title of champions for that year.

Progress to the 1969/70 Final was eventful. Then, as now, universities played one another in regional leagues in the initial part of the Competition. We competed in the North-east league, against Durham, Hull, York and Sheffield. There was another disappointing performance against a weaker Hull University side (see above) but this time it resulted in a narrow 6 – 3 win. *The Courier's* report commented that "Newcastle had so much possession that perhaps overconfidence was their chief undoing". However, Sheffield were beaten more convincingly, 22 – 0, and York were totally outplayed, 76

- 8. Unfortunately, we were beaten by Durham, and finished only second in the League. However, all was not lost, because the top two teams in each league proceeded to the knock-out stages of the Competition.

Loughborough (away) were the opponents in the quarter-final and they were beaten by one converted try, one try and one penalty goal (11 points) to one dropped goal and one penalty goal (6 points).

The semi-final was then played at Sheffield University's ground against University College, Aberystwyth. The conditions were atrocious and so, it would seem, were 'Father' Woodcock's navigational skills! *The Courier's* report commented:

Courier

Woodcock's age reaches three figures as.....

RUGBY ARE U.A.U. FINALISTS FOR SECOND SUCCESSIVE YEAR

Newcastle University 8 points Aberystwyth 0 points

For the second successive year, the University 1st XV reached the U.A.U. Final with a win over Aberystwyth. This year's semi-final was played under one, two or three inches of snow (or thick frost as our Welshman calls it), depending on which newspaper you read.

Sheffield have once again managed to conceal their pitches in the suburban outback of Norton, so convincingly this time that even Father Woodcock couldn't find them. Still we were not alone in our search for the Aberystwyth coach was behind us. First victory to us!

The bright sun shining on the snow put a severe strain on the eyes and this probably accounted for the early unsure handling. Newcastle were more quickly on to their opponents' mistakes and with footrushes put the early pressure on Aberystwyth, evidence of which was provided by footprints in the snow. Several members went close to scoring but it was only when Aberystwyth retaliated that we realized that we needed some points. Roger Francis responded by scoring a try, which was converted by Alan Towersey.

The second half was dominated by kicking. However, this emphasized the difference between the sides, for while we were kicking for position, Aberystwyth kicked because they had no other ideas behind the scrum.

Jim Partridge collected one wild clearing kick and ran diagonally to link with the rest of the three- ▶

▶ quarter line to give Roger Frantic (i.e. Francis – ed.) another try. The conversion failed. We now expected Aberystwyth to run the ball but we were disappointed mainly because our pack won most of it. The nearest they got to scoring was four long and hopeful penalty attempts.

With our six supporters cheering even more loudly we contained them until the final whistle and prepared for the important business of Anglo-Welsh hospitality.

Sale (Manchester) was agreed as the venue for the final. The Rugby Club hoped to take down coach-loads of supporters to counter the 'thousands of screaming fans that the rugby-mad Welshmen are sure to bring with them'. While this objective was not fulfilled and Newcastle supporters were in the minority at the match, they by no means let the side down. It seems that they accounted very well for themselves in the off the pitch battle.

A major disappointment for Newcastle was that flanker Dave Woodcock was forced to withdraw from the team. He had torn knee ligaments in an earlier club match. This was Dave's eighth and final season playing for the University – he had completed a BSc in Chemistry, a Masters' degree, a PhD and a Certificate in Education. Not a mean collection of trophies to go with his achievements on the rugby field! The Club felt that Dave's experience and ability to read a game would be sorely missed. There was also real disappointment that he would not play in what was likely to be the highlight of his rugby career.

The final itself ended in a 12 points-all draw. The brief report in *The Courier* read:

Ageless! Dave Woodcock, former captain and highly experienced member of the 1st XV

Courier

RUGBY SHARE UAU TITLE AFTER TITANIC TUSSLE IN SALE'S MUD

The 1st XV played the UAU Rugby Final last Wednesday and led a bunch of marauding Welshmen to an exciting draw. When I said led, I don't mean by the nose but by the score – the lads were never behind. Some impressive kicks by Cowman accounted for our score. Leading 12–9 three minutes before the end, an unfortunate penalty gave the Welshmen a chance to equalise which they did.

Extra time was played and both sides had chances nipped in the bud. No more scores in extra time meant a draw. It was a hard and fair match and I think that both sides were glad to come away with honours even.

It was a good game and, although in some ways it was disappointing, the lads did it – we did win the UAU!

John Pargeter gave a more detailed account in *The Journal* on Thursday 12th March:

THE JOURNAL

Newcastle share trophy after battle in the mud

Newcastle University 12pts
University College Bangor 12pts

Newcastle and Bangor fought out a marathon final to the British Universities' Rugby Championships at Sale yesterday, and, fittingly, the scores were level after extra time so that they share the trophy and the title.

It was Newcastle's first success in this event in the seven years that they have been a separate university, though they were runners-up last year.

The match was played on a quagmire pitch and when the players turned round for extra time it was barely possible to recognise the jerseys let alone the individuals.

The referee's task became ▶

difficult, as indeed, did that of the players, who floundered somewhat in the stamina-testing extra 20 minutes, the wisdom of which the Sale club must be doubting for it made an awful mess of the pitch.

Nevertheless, Newcastle had the better of extra time, though paradoxically Bangor should have scored, missing a penalty, which earlier in the game they would surely have converted.

With Newcastle's supporters outnumbered about 10 to one, the vocal encouragement by the Welsh can be imagined, and no doubt helped them to equalise only three minutes from the end of extra time.

From Newcastle's point of view this was a bitter blow, for they had led all along 3 – 0, 6 – 0, 6 – 3, 6 – 6, 9 – 6, 12 – 6 – half-time –

12 – 9, 12 – 12.

With so much crowd distraction and such a gluepot of a surface, play did not attain any heights. Rather, it was destructive. At times, there was little control and the players too became over-excited.

Yet the entire 100 minutes were full of excitement as chances galore were missed.

Obviously it was not easy to run with the ball and continuity was sadly lacking. The order of the day was to kick, and over the whole match I thought that Newcastle did it slightly better.

Remarkably, Bangor looked the more dangerous when they ran it out and they did have the satisfaction of scoring the only try, all other points coming from penalties.

The 1969/70 Joint Holders of the Universities Athletic Union Championship. The captain was Clive Goatman

Seven-a-side experts

Seven-a-side tournaments were extremely popular in the 1960s and 1970s, attracting big crowds. Young, fit and skillful student sides did well in them and, as King's College, we had won the Northumberland County Tournament in 1951/52 and 1954/55, and the Durham County Sevens in 1955/56.

Newcastle University continued this fine record with three further Northumberland County wins:

1965/66. Ashington were defeated 21 – 0 in the first round and then Old Novos 21 - 5 in the quarter-final. The semi-final was a closely contested affair against sevens specialists Morpeth. They were eventually defeated 6 - 0. Northern were overwhelmed in the final 30 – 3, the largest margin ever in the final of the competition in its 37-year history.

1967/68. Rockcliff were beaten 13 – 5 in the first round, followed by Northern, 18 – 0. However, there was a potential problem against Tynedale in the semi-final described as follows in *The Courier*:

Courier

Bloody Woodcock leads his men to victory

Against Tynedale near tragedy struck. Brave Captain Woodcock went down with a head injury. But – Oh how gallant! – he played on. Yes, he played on even with his head swathed in masses of bloody bandage. A score of 13 – 6 saw the team to the Final.

Now our noble Captain had a dilemma and three or four yards of bandage over his head. Reserves there were in plenty. But – and I think that we can be frank about this – they were all drunk. So the Captain played on disregarding advice – which I personally think was ridiculous – about the impossibility of a head transplant on the grounds of tissue rejection.

And the mighty Gosforth went down 27 – 5! The vociferous crowd reached and maintained an unprecedented volume of noise and the team reacted by turning on a glorious performance – scoring almost at will. The presenter of the Trophy – an eminent personage - said it was the best display of sevens Rugby he had ever seen in the competition. And so it was. The Cup was filled some umpteen times and everybody lived happily ever after.

1969/70. The progression to the final, started with an exciting 14 - 10 victory over Middlesbrough, the previous year's winners of the competition, followed by two much easier victories against Northern Counties College (28 - 0) and Old Novos (23 - 5). In the final, Gosforth were our opponents again; they were beaten 20 - 10. This time the Newcastle Captain for the day, Roger Francis, was the hero. The winger pulled a hamstring five minutes into the match but still managed to score three tries.

Another achievement was that the Club hosted the Sevens event in 1966/67, holding it at the University's Sports Ground at Close House, Wylam. We were gracious enough as hosts not to win the Trophy on this occasion; Morpeth did so.

Players and personalities

It goes, almost without saying, that such success in both the 15-a-side and 7-a-side versions of the game can only be achieved with outstanding players. There were many of them.

Three Newcastle University players became internationals, two of them while they were still at university:

- Ken Goodall was a chemical engineer from Londonderry and an outstanding No 8, representing both Ireland and the British Lions. He had the qualifications to play for England, since his father was a Yorkshireman and he was born in Leeds. However, his Irish mother persuaded Ken's father that life was better in her home town of Londonderry. As a consequence, Ken was brought up in Ireland from the age of four onwards. While an undergraduate at Newcastle, he is quoted as saying:

  "So far as I am concerned, I am an Irishman and I want only to play for Ireland. I have got the impression that somehow I would not fit into the English scene. And anyway, the forward play is a lot harder in Ireland and that's the way I like it."

  Ken won his first of many Irish caps against Australia in January 1967.

86

- Brian Keen played as a prop for England, playing in each of the four internationals in the 1968/69. At 5ft 10½in and 14½ stone, he was regarded as being small for an international prop but compensated by being one of the toughest and fastest in this position in the country. He was an outstanding footballer, and as a fresher he started playing for one of the college sides as full back. He was good enough to be selected in his first game for the University 1st XV in that position. Interestingly, many years later (in the mid-1980s) he turned out as a centre for a Vice-Presidents' XV against the University 3rd XV.

England international prop, Brian Keen. Photo courtesy of The Journal

England international stand-off, Dick Cowman. Photo courtesy of Dave Woodcock

- Dick Cowman was England's stand-off half, after leaving the University with a degree in Chemistry and joining Coventry. He had been 'discovered' by the University playing inter-mural rugby for Henderson Hall and evidently had to be persuaded that there was an outstanding career in rugby in front of him.

Dave Woodcock was a highly influential player for much of this era. His 'advanced' years were something he was never allowed to forget. It was a regular source of fun in articles in *The Courier*:

In discussing the promise of the 1968/69 season:

> The injection of new talent from the Freshers plus some old hands, Dave Woodcock being the oldest of them all, will weld an effective unit far more quickly than in previous years.

And after a win but poor team performance against Percy Park:

> It is hard to cook up any enthusiasm for the game. Suffice it is then to give the scores. Woodhenge (is he really so old?) got both tries – good ones.

And...

> And stalwarts return, during the holiday (not vacation please), Woodcock now in his 17th season and as fresh as ever, completed his metamorphosis into a Viking whilst drinking his way through Ireland.

And finally an apology...

> The Sports Editor would like to apologise for a misprint which appeared in last week's rugby column. Dave Woodcock is not now in his 17th season. The correct figure should have been 27.

Several members of the Club were awarded County caps during this period, including John Tarbit, Dick Cowman, Ken Sykes, John Seymour, Stu Masheder and Brian Keen.

7

DURHAM RIVALRY;
AND THE DREAM FINAL THAT
BECAME A NIGHTMARE

A 'derby' of all 'derbies'

The inevitable rivalry with Durham University following the separation of the two universities became a reality from the first match between the two clubs in 1963/64. They were scheduled to meet each other once only during the season – a fixture in the North-eastern League of the UAU Championship. This was always the big match, with massive commitment from the players and large (up to 2,000) partisan spectators, by no means all of whom were students. Interest in the match is illustrated, for example, by the build-up to the match in 1965-66, which prompted the following article in *The Courier*:

Courier

Rugger fans will invade Durham

Durham townsfolk will get a shock next Wednesday when the Cathedral city is flooded by chanting Newcastle students.

For next Wednesday is the day of the Rugby 'derby' between Newcastle and Durham universities when several hundred supporters will bear down on Durham in 'coach-convoy' for what has been termed a 'Crowd-in on Durham'.

Robin Poyntz, Captain and hooker of the Rugby Club, was very encouraged at the spirit that is building up for the big match. "We need every supporter we can get for this match. It's going to be very close, especially being at Durham. I put our chances at 50:50. If we outnumber them on the touchline, as I am sure we will, I'll say a win".

Coaches have been organised by the Rugby Club in response to the overwhelming Durham contingent at Cochrane Park last year when the visitors dominated the touchline. Durham won that match 17 – 6.

So retaliation has really set in this year. Posters have been distributed around the University, at the RVI and General Hospital, and Kenton Lodge Teachers' Training College. A great proportion of support will come from the fairer sex. Tickets can be obtained for the dance that will be held at Durham City Rugby Club that night.

However, one ardent supporter is a doubtful candidate for the match. This is the Captain's two-week-old baby daughter. Reports come from the hospital that she is in good vocal form – which might have proved useful on the touchline.

Durham and Newcastle compete for line-out ball at the Racecourse Ground, Durham. Photo courtesy of Dave Woodcock

Robin Poyntz was to be disappointed. Durham won that match by a penalty goal, arising from a late tackle, to nothing. However, Poyntz would have his revenge because a Durham – Newcastle play-off was needed that season to decide the League's winners: Newcastle won it by an even closer margin – by two points!

Other season's results in league matches were:

1963/64	Durham 19	Newcastle 3
1964/65	Newcastle 6	Durham 17
1965/66	Durham 3	Newcastle 0
Play-off	Durham 9	Newcastle 11
1966/67	Newcastle 9	Durham 3
1967/68	Durham 11	Newcastle 3
1968/69	Newcastle 10	Durham 0
1969/70	Durham 9	Newcastle 3

Not surprisingly, *The Courier* tended to concentrate on Newcastle wins. The narrow win in 1966/67 was described as:

> MAGNIFICENT is the only word to describe the University's performance against Durham in the local derby on Wednesday.
>
> ...the forwards played like men inspired.

The Courier's correspondent went gloriously over the top, even for *The Courier*, following the 10 – 0 Newcastle victory two years later:

Courier

RUGBY CHAMPS – AS THEY DESTROY RIVALS
Newcastle 10   Durham 0

Bismarck said in 1864 that the issues of the day would be settled by 'iron and blood'; and Churchill once mentioned 'blood, sweat and tears'.

Apt words indeed for as ▶

▶ the hands of the pavilion clock crept slowly towards 4:38; as twilight further darkened a dank, gloomy day even further; as 30 players pushed bruised limbs to limits of exertion; as tension in the vociferous crowd rose to fever pitch; as 'steam' rising from scrums combined with the Tyne's mist to produce a fairy-tale atmosphere; then the issues of the day were finally settled – and in Newcastle's favour!

Further progress in the UAU in 1968/69

Despite Durham's 0 – 10 loss to Newcastle, and therefore their position as runners-up in the Northern League, they were not out of the Championship. The rules of the Competition were changed from that season onwards so that winners and runners-up in each League proceeded to the knock-out stages. With typical tenacity, Durham took the fullest advantage of this opportunity and were to progress right through to the final. First, they crushed a fancied Leeds University team 21 – 3 in what was described as their most fluent performance for seasons. Then they overcame Bristol, 9 – 5 in the quarter-final. Semi-final opponents, UWIST (University of Wales Institute of Science and Technology) were beaten 20 – 12, with English international full-back Rossborough scoring 17 of their points.

Meanwhile, Newcastle were progressing in the other side of the draw.

Dead or alive? Two players causing concern in the Newcastle versus Sussex match which was played under appalling conditions. Photo courtesy of Dave Woodcock

Manchester University provided the first hurdle, and they were beaten 14 – 0.

However, there has inevitably been some feature or incident of special interest when Newcastle University reached the latter stages of competitions and this was the case in each of the three remaining rounds of the Competition. In the case of the quarter-final, in which Sussex University, winners of the Southern League, were the opponents, the weather was the problem. Sussex were defeated in atrocious conditions at Cochrane Park. John Pargeter writing in *The Journal* described it:

THE JOURNAL

Newcastle revel in the mud

Newcastle University 12pts   Sussex University 0

Rugby is a winter sport and, as such, players must be prepared to face the worst of the weather, but this Universities' Championship Quarter-final was almost farcical.

Long before half-time the players were simply grotesque figures clawing in the mud, and at one stage referee K S Lockerbie called both captains to him.

It was learned afterwards that he had asked if either team had a spare set of jerseys and, with a negative answer, he then asked to bear with him if he made a mistake, for it was impossible for him on the spot to distinguish the individual strips, even though they started with Newcastle in blue and Sussex in white with a narrow red hoop.

They must have been astounded too by the fact that Newcastle managed to score four tries – and all after good handling! In fact, had the surface been firm, I fancy that Newcastle would have won by a large margin. They were more mobile forward and much more skilful behind.

The victory was the more praiseworthy in that West, a Newcastle winger, was hurt in the first few minutes, and Moriarty, a second row forward, after 15. Both limped on but were just a nuisance value.

Newcastle's line-up for the semi-final against University College, Aberystwyth included Ken Goodall. He had been picked for Ireland on the following Saturday and this led to some gamesmanship from Aberystwyth beforehand. It was described by Bob Harrison in the *Evening Chronicle*:

EVENING CHRONICLE

The game was originally scheduled for either Wilmslow or Broughton Park but, when neither ground was available, the UAU suggested a week's postponement when Broughton Park would be available.

Aberystwyth objected to this because they felt that this would allow Ken Goodall, Newcastle's Irish international, to play, whereas he was unlikely to play on the original date because of the Irish-England international three days later.

Aberyswyth had their way and the game reverted to the original date but at a different venue, Loughborough. Our opponents' attitude probably strengthened Ken's resolve to play for Newcastle but, rather than risk the wrath of the Irish selectors, he elected to play anonymously. John Pargeter's report in *The Journal* read:

THE JOURNAL

Goodall fools selectors

Newcastle University 17pts   Aberystwyth University 6pts

One of the stars of Newcastle's exciting win was Ken Goodall, the Irish international who played under a false name.

He appeared on the programme as "M Butcher".

"I was terribly keen to play," he said, "but the Irish selectors might have forbidden it, so I kept quiet."

He plays for Ireland against England this weekend.

With less than 10 minutes to go the score was 6 – 6 and the match was heading towards an awkward draw.

At this stage Newcastle used a pre-arranged tactical move when awarded a penalty, scored a try, converted it, and then added another six points as Aberystwyth panicked.

Over the whole piece, Newcastle were worth an even bigger win. The Welsh forwards were all about the same size – barrel-shaped – and, showing no faith in their backs after a couple of bone-shaking tackles by their Newcastle counter-parts, they confined play to the pack, with the fly-half simply kicking.

Above: Line-out action in the semi-final against Aberystwyth.
Photo courtesy of Dave Woodcock

Below: Ken Goodall (occasionally alias M Butcher) watches as Willie John McBride wins line-out ball for Ireland against Wales. At that time, Ken was reputedly the best No 8 in the world. Photo courtesy of Inpho Photography

The national press reacted negatively to Goodall's pre-match tactics but Bob Harrison pointed out that he had not intended to conceal from the Irish RFU that he had played:

EVENING CHRONICLE

It was merely a move to avoid publicising the fact that he intended to play.

At any rate I liked the reply of the Irish RFU official when asked what he thought of Goodall turning out for Newcastle in midweek before an international.

He said Goodall was a free agent quite entitled to make his own decision in the matter.

After all, as the RFU are so keen to remind everyone, this is an amateur game; loyalties sometimes overlap and Ken Goodall acted in the truly traditional amateur manner.

The dream (?) final

The Newcastle – Durham Final was a great boost for rugby in North-east England, and aroused huge interest in the region. However, the first problem was in bringing the game to this part of the country. It had originally been scheduled for Manchester and, since it was the 50th year of the UAU, was to be followed by a celebration dinner. The first reaction was that these arrangements should remain but eventually common sense prevailed and the game was switched to Ashbrooke Stadium, home of Sunderland RFC. Supporters of both sides could now relish the prospect of the 'final of all finals'.

Regrettably however, misfortune was to strike Newcastle cruelly and in an almost unbelievable fashion. The Club started as favourites, especially after the convincing victory over Durham earlier in the season. But then Goodall suffered an ankle injury in the Scotland – Ireland international, and was out of action for the rest of the season so that he was unavailable. The first doubts in the Newcastle team began to appear. Bob McManners, 1st XV Captain, did his utmost to keep team confidence buoyant in an interview with the *Northern Echo*:

"We'll miss Goodall, there's no doubt about that but it's more psychological than physical. If we can forget we haven't got him with us then I'm sure we'll win. We have beaten them once and we can do it again."

Neither McManners nor anyone else could have had an inkling that Goodall's bad luck was only the first in a series of mishaps. Replacements were not allowed, even for injured players, in those days. Many matches were ruined because of injuries. The report of the final by Dave Thompson and Sam Swallow in the *Northern Echo* read:

Cowman breaks leg – and the Newcastle dream is ended

Reduced to 14 men after only nine minutes, Newcastle University failed in their bid to land the UAU final for the first time in the history of the competition when they were beaten 22 – 6 by a joyous Durham side at Sunderland's Ashbrooke Stadium yesterday.

Newcastle started favourites on the strength of a 10 – 0 win over Durham earlier in the season, but when Dick Cowman hobbled the long journey back to the pavilion with a broken leg most of their hopes went with him.

The game was a chapter of accidents – with Newcastle the principal sufferers. The skipper, Bob McManners, missed 15 minutes of the second half with concussion and was later taken to hospital. Ian Kerss played 75 minutes with a broken hand and had to be treated in hospital. The scrum half, Graham Partington, injured a shoulder early on, restricting his service to the

backs, and Roger Francis finished the game with several loose teeth.

It was not an especially dirty game. On the day that mattered the fates were with Durham who, to their credit, made the most of golden opportunities.

Durham opened the scoring after five minutes with a 60-yard penalty goal by Rossborough. Just after this, Cowman missed an attempted drop goal and it was from the resulting drop out he received his injury.

Newcastle were hastily re-arranged, Francis moving to fly half and Woodcock dropping out from openside to centre. Francis replied with a penalty goal to level at 3 – 3.

Durham scored their first try when Williams worked a scissors with Smith after 38 minutes. Rossborough missed the conversion and it was 6 – 3 at half-time. This was the first time Newcastle had conceded a try in the competition since October.

In the second half Durham

▶ had the territorial advantage. Newcastle, down to 13 men when McManners went off, were unable to cover as well as normal. Even so they attempted to move the ball about as much as possible.

After 20 minutes of the second half, McManners returned, but his presence still failed to prevent Durham from scoring more tries. These came from Buttle (2) and Pringle (2). All four tries came from combined forwards and backs moves which Newcastle, feeling their handicap, could not halt because of their deficit of men. Graham Partington replied with a dropped goal.

Outstanding in the Durham backs were John Regan and Rossborough at full-back. Both made dazzling runs. In the forwards, Pringle and Buttle played well. For Newcastle, all the forwards played well, gaining equal possession from the set pieces, with Ken White outstanding in the lineouts and Geoff Hales' crunching tackles a feature.

As John Pargeter commented in *The Journal*:

What a case this match could make for substitutes at all levels!

Although he may not have had in mind the small 'armies' of replacements that feature in modern matches!

8

FORGING AHEAD:
1970 – MID 1980s

Prior to the 1960s, the leading student sides had been a handful for most senior club sides because, although the forwards were lighter and less powerful than their opponents, their backs tended to be fitter, more skilful and better organised. Clubs depended on keeping the ball away from our three-quarters! The result was some wonderful matches between our own teams and the best of the local clubs, with the outcomes depending on the extent to which the students could score more points with 25% of the ball than their elders with 75% of it.

However, as rugby clubs began to take the game more and more seriously, skill, fitness and organisation levels improved, especially in the more ambitious ones. The 'traditional' advantages of student sides were being eroded. Furthermore, huge differences began to appear in the playing strengths of the more successful clubs and the less successful ones. Newcastle University had Saturday fixtures with all of the senior club sides in the region in the 1960s and early 1970s, although not necessarily in all seasons. The only senior club in the region that was not included in the fixture list was West Hartlepool, which was rapidly becoming the leading club in Durham, and indeed a leading national side. We had played, and often beaten, 'West' prior to the 1970s but regrettably games were not arranged thereafter.

The University now struggled against the top seven or eight clubs in the region. Although we were never disgraced in matches against them,

Above: Hair styles! The 1974/75 team photograph, with Stewart Evans – his first season as team manager

Below: More staff support. Four of the staff who supported the Club during the 1970s are shown here with Jeremy Weatherhead, Area Manager of Dryborough's Brewery (match sponsor). From left to right: Professor Tony Badger (Manager of Centaurs), Derek Nicholson (Registrar and Fixture Secretary), Weatherhead, Professor Keith Runcorn (President) and Bernard Jones (Coach)

invariably contributing to fast, open games of rugby, few of these games were won. However, the record needs to be put into perspective. We were still strong – but the best club sides were becoming ever stronger. For example, three wins out of 13 fixtures against Morpeth sounds poor but this was during a period when Morpeth were exceptionally strong. They even reached the quarter-finals of the Powergen Cup, beating the likes of Bath and London Irish on the way, and only going out to Rosslyn Park after a close and hard fought match.

Newcastle University's records against senior club sides in north-east England between 1970/71 – 1986/87. This analysis is based on the results of matches recorded in The Journal *over this period*

| | P | W | D | L | POINTS | | % wins |
					For	Against	
Seghill	10	7	0	3	168	89	70
Rockcliff	13	9	0	4	227	119	69
Carlisle	11	7	1	3	145	98	68
Novocastrians	14	7	0	7	192	175	50
Darlington	10	5	0	5	135	152	50
Gateshead Fell	13	6	0	7	156	197	46
Sunderland	13	5	0	8	144	227	38
Stockton	10	3	0	7	106	169	30
Percy Park	11	3	0	8	102	123	27
Tynedale	8	2	0	6	55	181	25
Alnwick	13	3	0	10	88	197	23
Morpeth	13	3	0	10	97	210	23
Northern	13	1	2	10	112	271	15
Westoe	7	1	0	6	85	175	14
Hartlepool Rovers	8	1	0	7	62	228	13
Blaydon	12	0	2	10	110	222	8
Middlesbrough	5	0	0	5	43	161	0
Durham City	7	0	0	7	48	228	0
Gosforth	5	0	0	5	10	205	0

Successes against the top clubs were sufficiently unusual to create comment in the press. Our single defeat of Northern in this period was in February 1986. It was a typical student – senior club side clash. Duncan Madsen described it in the *Evening Chronicle*:

EVENING Chronicle

University shock win

Newcastle University were worthy 14 – 13 winners over a lacklustre Northern side at Cochrane Park to pull off one of the biggest shock results in local rugby for a long time.

The University's tackling and back play were of a far higher standard and the winning try scored by Rhodes after an initial break by Petyt, and good work from Martin, was good enough to win any game.

Caswell, a sharp centre, opened the scoring for the University with an opportunist try, although the lead was soon wiped out by a similar effort from Clegg for Northern.

Walker then put Northern ahead with a try converted by Moffat and, despite an excellent try by Martin which reduced the lead at half-time to 10 – 8, Northern went further ahead shortly after the resumption with a Moffat penalty.

Hardie's conversion of Rhodes' try mid-way through the half restored the University's lead and, in the face of some naïve tactics from Northern, who had the lion's share of possession but were unable to use it, they never really looked like relinquishing it.

We were, nevertheless, still a match for many clubs, including several famous ones, such as Novocastrians, Darlington, Rockcliff and Carlisle. Our records against these clubs were much more encouraging.

The Journal Trophy

Overall, the table of results against north-eastern clubs (presented above) suggests that we were between about the 15th and 20th strongest side in the region – which was largely confirmed by our performances in The Journal Trophy. This competition, which started in the 1975/76 season, was run by *The Journal* newspaper. It was based only on matches that were played between teams in the League, and performance was assessed on percentage wins. There were 16 teams, including Newcastle University, in the League's first season. However, the League was gradually expanded and by 1982/83 numbers in it had roughly doubled. Two leagues, divisions 1 and 2, were then established. We were initially allocated to Division 2, and performed extremely badly in the first year, coming bottom of it. Nevertheless, two seasons later, we won the Division 2 trophy and were promoted to Division 1.

Performances of Newcastle University in The Journal Trophy.

Season	Number of teams in league	Position	P	W	D	L	Points for	Points against
A single league								
1975/76	16	14	10	3	0	7	115	154
1976/77	16	12	11	4	0	7	68	236
1977/78	20	20	13	1	0	12	77	278
1978/79	20	15	10	2	2	6	84	180
1979/80	22	19	14	3	1	8	121	215
1980/81	25	24	14	1	2	11	138	244
1981/82	25	24	18	2	1	15	155	296
League divided into two divisions (Newcastle University in Division 2)								
1982/83	15	15	11	1	0	10	59	197
1983/84	16	8	12	5	2	5	161	152
1984/85	20	1	11	10	0	1	188	69
League divided into two divisions (Newcastle University in Division 1)								
1986/87	19	19	13	0	1	12	80	264

County cup competitions

Unfortunately, the County decided to hold the Northumberland Senior Cup Competition at the end of the season so that all of the rounds were held during the Easter vacation. The Club withdrew from it rather than face the problems of bringing students back to Newcastle. This was with the exceptions of seasons 1982/83 and 1983/84, in which we did compete. However, the experiment was ill-fated. We were beaten in the first round on both occasions, losing to Seghill in the first of these seasons, and then Morpeth in the second.

The early rounds of other County competitions were played in term-time and Centaurs were able to compete. They were runners in the Senior Shield (second team competition) twice:

1971/72. Centaurs lost 3 – 9 to Berwick in the final but had dispatched Gosforth Greyhounds (their second team) in the semi-final.

1973/74. Centaurs beat Northern Wanderers (second team) 16 – 9 in the semi-final but lost 6 – 25 to Gosforth Greyhounds in the final.

Centaurs also reached the semi-final in 1974/75, losing 0 – 9 to North Shields 1st XV.

The Club hosted the Northumberland Sevens at Cochrane Park in 1982. Gosforth won the Competition, with Newcastle University runners-up. We won the County Seven-a-side Plate in 1986.

Performances in university competitions

Throughout this period in our history the 1st XV was almost invariably strong by comparison with most other universities but was only occasionally very good. Overall, we can probably bracket ourselves with universities such as Bristol, Nottingham, Leeds and Manchester, but were over-shadowed (as was everyone else) by Durham and Loughborough, who dominated the inter-universities (UAU) championship during this period.

Newcastle almost always reached the knock-out stages of the championship and progressed to the semi-final twice and the final once. The two semi-final appearances were:

1971/72

Runners-up to Durham University in the Northern Division, having beaten Hull 22 – 4 and Sheffield 24 – 6, but lost to Durham 6 – 12.

First qualifying round: won.

Quarter-final: beat Swansea 6 – 0.

Semi-final: lost to Bristol 6 – 13.

1972/73

Runners-up to Durham University in the Northern Division, having beaten Hull 12 – 3 and Sheffield 19 – 3, but lost to Durham 0 – 4.

First qualifying round: beat Leeds 22 – 15.

Quarter-final: beat Bristol 3 – 0.

Semi-final: lost to Loughborough 9 – 30.

1976/77: UAU Finalists

The most successful season in this period of our history, started with a hiccup. Hull were normally beaten decisively but not so in October 1976. John Pargeter in *The Journal*:

THE JOURNAL

An early shock for 'Varsity

Hull Univ. 7pts Newcastle Univ. 3pts

Newcastle lost their first match in the Universities' Rugby Championship yesterday in a game of mixed fortunes from their point of view.

For they scored first with a penalty by skipper Currie.

However, the home forwards began to dominate in both line-out and scrummage, and only close covering by the Newcastle back row, and good clearances by full-back Clarkson prevented Hull scoring.

In the second half, the Newcastle three-quarters showed promise, half-backs Wright and Campbell featuring, but the game was interrupted frequently by the referee so neither side could get clean ball moving.

Hull scored a try after a long run and this was the end for Newcastle, and Hull widened the margin with a penalty.

Sheffield, our next opponents, this time at home, were caught on the rebound. They were soundly beaten 53 – 12.

Our great rivals, Durham University, were the next visitors to Cochrane Park, and they too were beaten, leaving us as divisional winners and qualifiers for the knock-out part of the competition. Pargeter's report in *The Journal* summarised the match:

THE JOURNAL

Blow for Durham

Durham were beaten at Cochrane Park yesterday in the Universities' Rugby Championship, but they may look on it as a good omen!

The last time that this happened – eight years ago – Durham went on to win the national title.

Durham, then as now, went forward as group runners-up, and won all their matches – as did Newcastle – so they met in the final which, by arrangement, was played at Sunderland where Durham won!

At the start, Newcastle pushed Durham all over the place and generally subjected them to tremendous pressure, but they wasted their chances, holding when they should have passed, and kicking when passing seemed the answer.

They also missed three penalty kicks, and led only through a penalty through Clarkson.

Durham then took over, but they also missed a penalty, Bolam was just short after a fine run, Norkett was far too selfish, but eventually they gave the ball quickly to Womersley who ran well for a fine try, which Norkett converted.

Surprisingly, Durham did not play on Newcastle's right flank where Currie was hobbling about, but they were able to get more parity up front when Rennison damaged ribs.

The decisive score came a minute from normal time when Clarkson linked with Jarvis who made a spectacular run down the left flank to dive over and Clarkson made a magnificent conversion.

Final table:

	P	W	L	F	A	Pts
Newcastle	3	2	1	65	25	4
Durham	3	2	1	65	38	4
Hull	3	1	2	32	57	2
Sheffield	3	1	2	38	80	2

Manchester were beaten 27 – 3 in the first round of the knock out competition, followed by Bristol 12 – 6, in a game played under atrocious conditions. John Pargeter commented:

THE JOURNAL

Clarkson is spot on

Newcastle University reached the semi-finals of the Universities' Rugby Championship yesterday when they won at Cochrane Park by four penalty goals to two.

Newcastle thoroughly deserved their victory, thanks to some tremendous kicking by Joe Clarkson, their full-back.

Conditions were wretched, indeed only superhuman efforts by the ground-staff made the game possible, and then it rained. To make matters worse there was a strong wind!

Yet Clarkson kicked all four penalty goals, two of them into the wind, while Bristol could manage only two, both when the wind was in their favour.

Joe Clarkson

Joe Clarkson was beginning to make the tournament his own. John Pargeter was equally ecstatic about his performance in the semi-final, against University of Wales Institute of Science and Technology, who were coached by the legendary Welsh coach Carwyn James.

Joe Clarkson, in action for USA Eagles. He played as stand-off for the Eagles but was full-back for Newcastle University, Northern and Northumberland. Photo courtesy of Rugby USA

THE JOURNAL

Clarkson does it again

Newcastle University 6pts
University of Wales Institute of Science and Technology 4pts

The strong UWIST side was without current international forward Graham Price, injured against France on Saturday, but they took the lead after only eight minutes when right winger John Holt went over in the corner.

With driving rain making any attempts at open rugby almost impossible, the game developed into a forward struggle.

Newcastle were always looking to use their backs but in the first half, playing against the wind, they did not have one clear chance.

Instead, they began to rely on penalties, though when four kickable ones were missed before the interval, they must have worried about their chances of making the final.

Conditions, if anything, deteriorated but Newcastle slowly began to look impressive. Their passing became more fluent, and their kicking more accurate.

UWIST did not look like adding to their lead and it was only a matter of time before Newcastle closed the gap.

The first penalty came 10 minutes into the half, following a hack through – a ploy both sides might have made more use of throughout. A UWIST player infringed at the resultant ruck, and Clarkson made no mistake from under the posts.

Urged on by their band of supporters, Newcastle were rewarded about 15 minutes later when the Welsh scrum-half, Jones, fed his hooker, Maxstead. Clarkson slotted home the penalty.

Once ahead, Newcastle did not allow the cup-holders back into the game and with Clarkson hitting a post and the bar with subsequent penalty attempts, the victory margin could well have been larger.

After the match we needed to inform our President Professor Keith Runcorn of the situation. He was working at Cape Canaveral at the time so we sent him a telegram. In an attempt to reduce costs, we used the minimum number of words. It read:

NEWCASTLE6UWIST4FINALTWICKENHAM21MARCH1500.THELADS.

Keith was told by the NASA Operations Room that a telegram had arrived for him but that it was in code and, in spite of their best efforts, they had been totally unable to decipher it!

Regrettably, we failed at the final hurdle but, once again, we were plagued by extraordinary ill fortune. The team stayed overnight at Windsor before the match and left in plenty of time before kick-off. Kit was stowed in the boot of the coach but for reasons of its own the boot lid opened en route depositing centre Chris Fincher's kit on the road. The coach stopped 400 metres up the road from the incident and the players watched in horror as a motorist pulled up next to the abandoned kit, deposited it in the boot of his own car and drove off. Attempts to find a sports shop where Chris could buy replacement boots were abortive, and the team arrived at Twickenham flustered, with only 30 minutes to spare before kick-off.

Even then the drama had not ended. Chris did not expect to play, and substitute Peter Ashcroft was told that he would be replacing him – he actually appeared in the pre-match team photograph. At that time replacements were allowed only in the case of injury. Nevertheless, one of Loughborough's replacements generously offered Chris the use of his boots (foregoing his own chance to play should there be an injury), and Chris was back in the team.

The shortest appearance ever? Replacement Peter Ashcroft (third Newcastle player from the left in the back row) appears in the team photograph of the UAU finalists at Twickenham in 1977. Centre Chris Fincher, who actually played, is not shown because we were still sorting out a problem with his kit!

What a way to prepare for the match of a decade! The irony was that we were at least as good as Loughborough but were simply blown away in the first 20 minutes. John Pargeter described it in *The Journal*:

THE JOURNAL

Students fail with honours

Loughborough Colleges 23pts, Newcastle University 3pts

Newcastle didn't have a look-in during the first half of the University Rugby Championships final at Twickenham yesterday and were beaten by two goals, two tries and a penalty goal to one penalty.

For the first 40 minutes it was like lambs to the slaughter as the highly-organised Loughborough, having the advantage of the wind as well, twisted Newcastle in knots to score 23 points. It was a total Newcastle had no chance of wiping off despite a gallant display after the interval winning the second half 3 – 0.

In this period, Loughborough were most un-enterprising and disappointing and most of the aggression came from Newcastle.

In the first half, however, Loughborough were able to wheel the scrums when it suited them; they rucked magnificently and if their backs were not brought into the game it was only because it was an unnecessary risk.

It was Loughborough's 15th win in the last 25 finals and their fourth in the last five – figures which speak for themselves.

Rivalry with Durham University

The annual Durham match was regarded each season as the most important game of the season. Therefore only one win and one draw in 17 fixtures makes depressing reading. However, none of these matches were ever seen as a walkover by our opponents. Rivalry was as intense as ever, and we invariably gave a good account of ourselves but, each season, expectations were raised and then hopes were dashed for yet another year!

Results of matches against our rivals Durham

Season	Result	Score		Season	Result	Score
1970/71	L	3 – 20		1979/80	L	3 – 16
1971/72	L	6 – 12		1980/81	L	3 – 21
1972/73	L	0 – 4		1981/82	L	3 – 19
1973/74	L	7 – 16		1982/83	L	15 – 19
1974/75	L	12 – 16		1983/84	L	13 – 32
1975/76	L	6 – 20		1984/85	L	12 -15
1976/77	W	9 – 6		1985/86	L	3 – 20
1977/78	L	3 – 23		1986/87	L	7 – 8
1978/79	D	9 – 9				

The truth was that Durham were too good for us during this period. It was a time during which they dominated the UAU competition, including a period of four titles in five years, three of them in a row. However, as Ted Wood, the Durham coach over this period (and much more) warmly acknowledges, the Newcastle match was regarded as the fiercest of the season and one that, taken lightly, would have been at Durham's peril.

Fixtures against Durham are always keenly contested. The Newcastle pack prepares to scrummage. Photo courtesy of Tom McNicholas

Ted Wood was the architect of Durham University's fine achievements, and is still a major factor in the Club's continued success.
Photo courtesy of Ted Wood

The problem, as far as Newcastle were concerned, was that these Durham teams always included players that either already were or were about to become household names in the game, including the likes of Phil de Glanville, Will Carling, Andy Mullins, Chris Oti, Mark Bailey and Fran Clough. They were simply superb.

Outstanding personnel

John Stevens was the Club's first dedicated coach, taking over in 1978 when he took up a post in the Centre for Physical Recreation and Sport. John was instrumental in bringing about organisational changes in the Club, and improvements in playing facilities, including the installation of floodlights on the training pitch at Cochrane Park. Bernard Jones, a Lecturer in Physical Education, replaced him in 1983, remaining 'in charge' until 1998. He ensured that the Club functioned very much as a Club, with excellent, but not invasive, support from the Centre for Physical Recreation and Sport.

There were several excellent players in Newcastle's colours in this period. Full internationals caps were won by:

Dave Caplan who represented England at full back against France and Scotland in 1977/78.

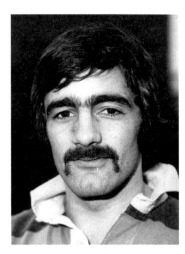

English international full-back and former 1st XV captain, Dave Caplan.
Photo courtesy of The Journal

Joe Clarkson, who emigrated to the United States and was capped by the USA Eagles on five occasions: against Japan (twice), Tunisia, Canada and England. He represented them at stand-off, although he had played at full-back for Newcastle University and the Northumberland County side.

John Jeffrey, an open-side flanker, who was knick-named the 'White Shark' because of his fair hair and predatory nature. He won numerous caps for Scotland and also toured with the Lions.

Other outstanding players were Paul O'Donnell, who represented Ireland B at stand-off, Hugh Parker, who played for Scotland 'A' as a lock,

'The White Shark' John Jeffrey of Agrics, Newcastle University, Kelso, Scotland and British Lions. In an interview, J J described Agrics as his favourite rugby club.
Photo courtesy of Associated Sports Photography

and Paul Sidi (hooker) who was a member of the England squad, without actually being capped.

In addition, several players represented Northumberland or other county teams. They include: Andy Cutter, Max Stone, John Blissett, Nigel Wright, Sandy McCrae, Paul Scott and Richard Petyt.

9

GETTING SERIOUS.
THE NATIONAL LEAGUES:
1987 – 1991

Survival and the leagues

The advent of national leagues in 1987/88 presented a major challenge to universities. We had seemingly been ignored in the new structure. League matches were scheduled to be played on fixed dates and approximately half of these dates were Saturdays during university vacations. It would be particularly difficult for us to fulfill fixtures in September or early October because players had vacation commitments (often associated with their studies). Furthermore, there was little opportunity for team 'get-togethers' or training sessions and, at that stage in the season, we were largely unaware of our new Fresher intake. At best, we could only field scratch teams.

Nevertheless, we entered the league system and believe that we were the only senior English university club to do so, although Loughborough Students and Hartpury Students have subsequently entered and now play in the leagues. Newcastle University's Medicals also entered the leagues, playing two tiers below us, in Durham and Northumberland League Division 2. However, since Medicals has become an open club, it does not face the problem that would eventually defeat us of fielding strong sides during vacations. Edinburgh University compete in the Scottish National Leagues and University of Wales Institute, Cardiff (UWIC) do so in the Welsh Leagues.

We were allocated to North-east Division 2, which was dominated by teams from Yorkshire. This was a bonus because it extended our Saturday fixture list, which had previously been confined almost entirely to Durham and Northumberland, to a range of new clubs. There were 11 teams in each division, and seven of those in North-east 2 were new fixtures. Teams were (then) due to play one another once only in the season.

However, the difficulties for us of playing early season matches were soon emphasised. By early October of the first (1987/88) season, before the academic year had started, we had already played, and lost, four matches

Chris Jones, captain in 1986/87, watches as the opposition's hooker throws into a line-out. Photo courtesy of The Journal

(almost half of the league fixtures). Our record read:

Played 4; Won 0; Drawn 0; Lost 4; Points for 24; Points against 98

We were well and truly bottom of the League. Once we were organised, fortunes changed. Three of the final six matches were won and we finished with the more respectable record of:

Played 10; Won 3; Drawn 0; Lost 7; Points for 123; Points against 191

We were no longer bottom of the League and survived in North-east 2 for a second season.

The pattern was repeated in subsequent seasons – matches played in vacations were lost and most of those played in term-time were won. The final tables for each of the four seasons in which we took part are as follows:

Season: 1987/88

	P	W	D	L	pts
Novos	10	9	1	0	19
Stockton	10	9	0	1	18
Pontefract	10	6	1	3	13
Hymerians	10	6	0	4	12
Beverley	10	5	0	5	10
Selby	10	4	0	6	8
York	10	4	0	6	8
Ryton	10	3	0	7	6
Pocklington	10	3	0	7	6
Newcastle Uni	10	3	0	7	6
Barnsley	10	2	0	8	4

Season 1988/89

	P	W	D	L	pts
York	10	8	1	1	17
Selby	10	7	1	2	15
Roundhegians	10	6	2	2	14
Pontefract	10	5	1	4	11
Beverley	10	5	0	5	10
Newcastle Uni	10	5	0	5	10
Ripon	10	4	0	6	8
Blyth	10	3	1	6	7
Hymerians	10	3	0	7	6
Ryton	10	3	0	7	6
Pocklington	10	3	0	7	6

Season: 1989/90

	P	W	D	L	pts
Bramley	10	10	0	0	20
Roundhegians	10	8	0	2	16
Westoe	10	7	0	3	14
Beverley	10	6	0	4	12
Pontefract	10	5	0	5	10
Ripon	10	4	0	6	8
Blyth	10	4	0	6	8
Hymerians	10	4	0	6	8
Newcastle Uni	10	4	0	6	8
Rockcliff	10	2	0	8	4
Ryton	10	1	0	9	2

Season 1990/91

	P	W	D	L	pts
West Park	10	8	0	2	16
Pontefract	10	7	0	3	14
Hymerians	10	5	2	3	12
Selby	10	5	1	4	11
Westoe	10	4	2	4	10
Blyth	10	5	0	5	10
Rockcliff	10	3	2	5	8
Beverley	10	4	0	6	8
Ashington	10	3	1	6	7
Ripon	10	3	0	7	6
Newcastle Uni	10	3	0	7	4*

Two points were deducted in 1990/91 because the Club did not fulfil a fixture in the Easter vacation.

Our best performance was in the season 1988/89. However, one victory, over Beverley, could be attributed to the fact that Cochrane Park was still in use for cricket when the match was due to be played in September. The rugby pitches overlap with the cricket outfield and, since the pitches had not been marked out and the posts had not been erected, rugby was not feasible. Under the circumstances, the League authorities gave us permission to play the game later in the season, although we would lose home advantage being forced to travel to Yorkshire for it. The Beverley fixture had been played in September in the two previous seasons with comfortable wins for the Club side. While the Beverley Club readily accepted the situation in 1988/89, one of its supporters was less generous. He had the elevated position of being in charge of the bucket and sponge when the match did eventually take place, but also took every opportunity to express his displeasure that Beverley were having to play against our 'proper' first team. No one (from either side) took very much notice until a Newcastle player was injured and coach Bernard Jones went over to 'borrow' the bucket and sponge. He was told that bucket and sponge belonged to Beverley, and that Bernard could go and get his own! Fortunately, the player recovered without the assistance of the magic sponge and the Newcastle team went on to win an excellent match, played in equally good spirit. However, this sad gentleman was even less happy now that his team had lost, and he decided to use the precious contents of his bucket to douse Bernard. Thankfully, the gentleman's aim seemed to fit well with the rest of his character, and he missed. Bernard had a dry and comfortable journey back to Newcastle!

The death blow to our league aspirations came before the start of the 1991/92 season. The World Cup was due to be played in England in October and November 1991, and no league fixtures were scheduled for this period. This included a large slice of our term-time and the result was that almost all of our fixtures were due to be played in vacations. We had no option but to withdraw from the leagues and, as soon as we had made

Bernard Jones (on the right) who guided the Club over a period of more than 15 years. An outstanding achievement was in avoiding a bucket of cold water aimed in his direction at Beverley! He is protected here by John Bates and Stewart Evans. Photo courtesy of Glyn Davies

our decision, players' interest in league matches declined. Indeed, one fixture was not completed in the Easter Vacation of 1991, causing us to have two points deducted from our total. We then finished bottom of the league.

It is regrettable that our league experiment ended in this way. We had done our utmost to compete but we felt that the rugby authorities could have done much more to support student involvement. It should surely have been possible for the Rugby Football Union to devise a system that could cater for both clubs and universities. All that was needed was for flexibility in match dates so that universities could agree mutually acceptable dates on which to play the league fixtures with their opponents.

Matches with universities

There is some evidence that playing league rugby sharpened our performance against other university teams. We had several comprehensive wins over Hull and Leeds in UAU matches, and recorded a win over Durham after a long period of losses. It was not merely a win but that very rare event for any university side – a win on Durham University's Racecourse ground!

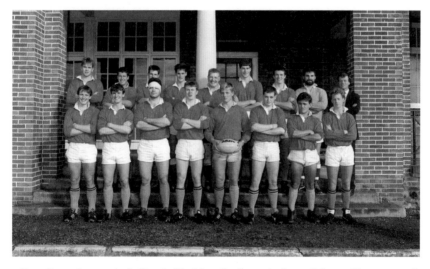

Dave Brown's team, including Paddy Johns (back row in front of the pavilion entrance), and Bernard Jones (on the right) in 1987/88. Peter Burrows, who is standing next to Bernard Jones, made over one hundred 1st XV appearances for the Club

Results of fixtures against Durham University

Season	Result	Score
1987/88	Lost	10 – 24
1988/89	Lost	12 – 15
1989/90	Won	16 – 13
1990/91	Lost	6 – 8

Jonathan Brewer was one of many Newcastle supporters who revelled in the 1989/90 match. His report in *The Courier* read:

Durham University.......... 13
Newcastle University....... 16

An exciting game by virtue of brilliant tries, controversial decisions and last-minute drama.

Not since 1976 have Newcastle beaten the old foe in the fifteen-man game, yet they played this one with cool, calm moves and some excellent finishing.

Durham opened the match with their usual power play but it was Newcastle who opened the scoring with a captain's penalty kick: Graeme Aitchison putting over after Ed Gregory had late-tackled Ali Witts.

Aitchison added three more points after Durham had conceded a penalty in the line-out and Newcastle looked set to go into half-time with a 6 – 0 lead. But this was not to be.

Durham contrived to drop the ball as they crossed the opposing goal-line but put points on the board when the referee awarded them a penalty try. Brian Dodds' controversial decision came after the Newcastle captain had his kick for touch charged down, the ball ballooning out to the Durham winger who was high tackled by Andy Graham.

Forty seconds into the second half and Durham struck again. The University were left shell-shocked when a stray pass was picked up by Durham's Phil Lecampe who went over making the score 6 – 10. Newcastle could have been down and out when Durham added three more points from a penalty, but they gritted their teeth and pushed forward.

Aitchison made up for some earlier penalty misses with a thunderbolt from the side- ▶

▶ line and, when Pete Kemble went over in the sixty-first minute, Newcastle could sense history in the making. At 12 – 13 Rich Uren just failed to push through a desperate Durham defence and the Newcastle lads watched as a drop goal attempt sailed just wide.

But with four minutes left, Newcastle's scrum-half, Tony Nickalls, scorched round the blind-side of a scrum on Durham's 22-yard line to nip through the opposition's defence to score a try.

Now that Durham were behind, they powered forward to save the game. However, two superb, last-man tackles from Graeme Aitchison stopped them just short of the line. A three point difference was just reward for a superb team performance.

Alex Munroe makes a break supported by Harry Clayton in the annual Durham 'derby'.
Photo courtesy of The Journal

Newcastle reached the quarter-final of the UAU Championship in three of these four seasons and the semi-final in one of them. The results of matches in the knock-out stages of the competition when the Club did not progress beyond the quarter-final were as follows:

Season 1987/88		
First round	Liverpool	12 – 6
Quarter final	Swansea	9 – 10

Season 1989/90		
First round	Sussex	42 – 3
Quarter final	Bristol	11 – 21

Season 1990/91		
First round	Lancaster	33 – 0
Quarter final	Warwick	9 – 12

The season 1988/89 was the most successful one of this era, especially when the Irish lock Paddy Johns, who went on to win 40 caps for his country, was playing. Once we had qualified for the knock-out stages of the UAU Competition, our progress towards the latter rounds was most impressive. Liverpool were beaten 19 – 3 in a preliminary round, and then Imperial College were dispatched 22 – 0. However, it was the destruction of Nottingham in the quarter-final that produced an outstanding display. Alan Hedley reported as follows in *The Journal* of 2 February 1989:

THE JOURNAL

Newcastle blitz destroys Notts

Newcastle University 26pts   Nottingham University 9pts

Newcastle University moved emphatically into the semi-finals of the UAU Championship with one of their best performances for several seasons at Cochrane Park.

It was in every sense a team effort yesterday. Newcastle hit Nottingham with a 16 points blitz in 19 minutes and they never recovered.

Paddy Johns playing at No 8 may have been judged man of the match but there were plenty of other candidates including full-back Graeme Aitchison, half backs Tony Nickalls and Rich Fisher, lock Harry Clayton and beavering back row forward John Jackson.

In fact, it is probably unfair to single out those players as there wasn't a Newcastle player who didn't play well.

Mike Shelley was an outstanding prop. Subsequently, he captained Leeds Tykes in the Premiership and now plays for Calgary Saints. He has played for England A. Mike is holding the trophy after captaining Leeds to victory in the Powergen final against Bath. Photo courtesy of Sportsbeat Images

Unfortunately, this form was not repeated in the semi-final. Paddy Johns was not in the team and the pack was further weakened when his second row partner Harry Clayton was injured. Alan Hedley summed up the match in *The Journal* as follows:

THE JOURNAL

Newcastle's Twickenham dream dies

Newcastle University 10   Swansea University 26

Newcastle University's dreams of their first trip to Twickenham since 1977 disappeared at Northampton yesterday.

Swansea adapted better to the quagmire of a pitch in this UAU semi-final, but Newcastle were nowhere near the side they were against Nottingham in the last round.

They also lost Harry Clayton in the 25th minute with a badly cut head and their scrummaging naturally suffered, and there was a real element of doubt about Swansea's first score.

But Newcastle's big failing was allowing Swansea too much leeway with the wind at their backs – and Newcastle chose to kick against it in the first half!

Newcastle got the worst possible start when Swansea kicked off with the strong wind and skipper Nick Johnson let it go, thinking it was headed straight into touch, but it bounced first and rolled out of play on the corner flag.

It signalled a period of immediate Swansea pressure and Newcastle were forced to put in some vital tackles.

They weren't helped by some indifferent touch kicking, fly-half Rich Fisher having a particularly difficult time against the strong wind.

Swansea full-back Richard Jones was just off target with a dropped goal shot after Fisher failed to make from his 22 and a minute later the Welsh were in front with a controversial score.

Fly-half Lee Evans put up a high kick and Newcastle fatally allowed it to bounce in the 22 and centre Andy Moore, who looked at least two yards in front of Evans when he kicked it, raced on to the ball to score.

Newcastle then settled down to play some steady stuff, but conceded a silly penalty in the 13th minute when Richard Uren did well to tackle Richard Mynott but then spoiled it by playing the ball before he got back on his feet and Evans kicked the penalty to make it 7 – 0.

Newcastle came back at the Welsh with a drive by Peter Burrows, Johnston and Tony Nickalls and Fisher had a drop goal shot half charged down.

Swansea forced play back down to the Newcastle line and again Newcastle tackling had to be spot on to stop the Swansea rolling maul.

But then Newcastle were hit by that injury to lock Clayton and while he was off and replacement Jim Parrott was coming on, Swansea seized their chance and drove Newcastle back at the scrum and Jaimie Devonald rocketed over for a try in the ▶

▶ corner in the 26th minute.

Newcastle must still have felt they were in with a chance, even at 11 – 0, with the wind to come in the second half.

But then they conceded a penalty going over the ball and Evans made it 14 – 0 on the half hour.

And right on half-time, there was a real killer blow when Swansea won three consecutive rucks. The ball was whipped out to Richard Jones and, sadly, Greg Smith missed the tackle for the full back to score in the corner.

Naturally, Evans kicked a great touchline conversion and the match suddenly looked well out of Newcastle's reach.

They needed a quick score in the second half but didn't get it.

Andy Lewin was short with a long range penalty, but it was Devonald who put Swansea well and truly on the road to Twickenham when he wrong-footed Graeme Aitchison – by far Newcastle's best player on the day – to score, Evans converting for a 26 – 0 scoreline nine minutes into the half.

To their credit Newcastle never gave up and Lewin brought off a marvellous try-saving tackle on Mynott, who was over the line when Lewin caught him and managed to get his hands on the ball at the touchdown for a 22 drop out.

Fisher missed a penalty for offside, but Newcastle rallied in the final quarter and Richard Uren looked to have scored when he broke through, but Swansea snapped up his inside pass when he was stopped on the line and somehow managed to clear.

Two tap penalty moves came to nothing, but a big drive at a maul saw prop Dai Lucas stopped on the line and Tony Nickalls was also hauled down on the line.

They kept up the pressure when Fisher cross kicked and the Newcastle pack drove Swansea back at the ensuing ruck for Nickalls to dive through for a try which Fisher converted.

With the final whistle only minutes away, Greg Smith hoisted a high kick and Swansea knocked on. From the scrum, Nick Johnson picked up and slipped the ball to flanker Dave Cherrington who burst through for a try.

10

THE DEMISE OF SATURDAY RUGBY
BUT NEW RIVALS: 1991 – 1996

Saturday Rugby

The withdrawal of the Club from the National Leagues had a negative impact on Saturday Rugby at Newcastle University. The Club's policy had always been that first and second team players were expected to commit themselves to both Wednesday and Saturday Rugby with the Club. There were occasional exceptions over the years, especially when we used players as replacements, but the feeling was that we gained more in club spirit from keeping the side together for Wednesdays and Saturdays than we lost in playing strength by bringing outside players into the Wednesday side. However, once we had come out of the National Leagues and could no longer offer League Rugby, most of our better players, who were more than willing to represent the University on Wednesdays, were now looking to improve themselves with outside clubs on Saturdays.

Saturday Rugby at Cochrane Park rapidly spiralled downwards. Not only did the quality of the team that we could field deteriorate but this was exacerbated because good fixtures were hard to come by. Club 1st XVs were heavily committed to the league matches so that, as our own playing standards diminished, we were forced to include matches against the lower teams of senior clubs and some junior clubs. Regrettably, we also saw a seamier side of rugby. It had always been accepted that matches against clubs would be hard and aggressive; it was part of the game. Clubs such as Gosforth, Northern, Alnwick, Tynedale, Morpeth, and those whom we had played in the national leagues, simply pitted their strengths against our own, resulting in wonderful games of rugby on the field and great camaraderie off it. However, on occasions, we now found ourselves fielding teams composed mainly of Freshers, straight out of school, against less fit and less skilful, but much larger men who seemed to have little on their minds other than 'student bashing'. We found it extraordinary that such a wonderful, inspirational, even beautiful game could, at times, deteriorate to such an ugly level!

The Club could see no value in playing fixtures of these kinds and the season, 1997/98, saw us at our lowest ebb – we decided to abandon Saturday fixtures concentrating solely on Wednesday, mostly university, Rugby. For the first time since the First World War, Cochrane Park was empty and silent on Saturday afternoons!

An empty Cochrane Park, in this case because it is mid-summer. However, the decline of club rugby on Saturdays in the late 1990s meant that for a time Cochrane Park was eerily silent on winter Saturday afternoons

Wednesday Rugby

Fortunately, Wednesday rugby continued in the same vein as before. We had a series of good sides, without reaching great heights. We always did well enough in the leagues to progress to the knock-out stages of the Universities' Championship, and reached the quarter-finals on three occasions. Results of the knock-out matches were as follows:

Season 1991/92		
Preliminary round	Aberystwyth	59 – 7
First round	Birmingham	26 – 19
Quarter-final	Durham	15 – 26

Season 1992/93		
First round	Cardiff	18 – 26

Season 1993/94		
First round	Crewe and Alsager	31 – 0
Quarter-final	University of Wales Institute Cardiff (UWIC)	15 – 37

Season 1994/95		
First round	Manchester	32 – 17
Quarter-final	Northumbria	7 – 21

Season 1995/96		
First round	Birmingham	7 – 15

The season 1992/93 was an interesting one because it saw the 'new' universities, former polytechnics, entering the competition for the first time. There was a huge range in the standard of their rugby teams. Sunderland were initially in the same league as ourselves in the inter-university competition but were out of their depth, losing 0 – 72 to us and by large margins in their other matches. However, Northumbria, who were in a division with Teesside, created an immediate impact. They were instantaneously one of the leading rugby universities, and were to become intense rivals, in some ways replacing Durham in this role.

Once they had been given university status, Northumbria University became major rivals. Several of the 1st XV matches have been played under floodlights either at Gateshead International Stadium or Kingston Park (home of Newcastle Falcons). Photo courtesy of The Courier

1993/94 saw a reorganisation of the divisional leagues in an attempt to avoid mis-matches. However they still occurred. Our record against other members of the division in that season illustrates the problem:

Bradford	69 – 9	Northumbria	7 – 34
Durham	15 – 24	Leeds	9 – 15
Leeds Metropolitan	61 – 5	Hull	walkover

Records against Durham and Northumbria were also disappointing in this period. There were many great games but somehow we were usually on the losing side. Nevertheless, Durham were beaten 15 – 6 in a League match in 1991/92. The two sides were then drawn to play one against another in the quarter-final of the knock-out stage, and this time Durham reversed the result, 15 – 26.

Results of the 'derby' matches during this period were:

Durham		
1991/92	W	15 – 6
1991/92 (QF)	L	15 – 26
1992/93	L	10 – 34
1993/94	L	15 – 24
1994/95	L	11 – 18
1995/96	L	8 – 16
1995/96	L	0 – 20

Northumbria		
1993/94	L	7 – 34
1994/95	L	12 -16
1994/95	L	7 – 21
1995/96	L	15 – 30
1995/96	L	10 – 27

Strength in depth

An encouraging trend during this disappointing era was that the Club began to show considerable strength in depth, a feature that was to be developed further in future years.

The 3rd XV reached the final of the Universities' Competition in 1992/93, achieving three victories of more than 80 points on their way there. However, they were well beaten by a strong Loughborough 3rd XV 15 – 37 in the final itself. The 3rd XV were also runners-up to Tynedale in the Northumberland County Third Team Competition in that season.

Winning clean line-out ball at Bullocksteads, Northumbria University's home ground. Photo courtesy of The Courier

In 1994/95, the 3rd XV won the BUSA Plate Final. *The Courier*'s match report was:

Warwick University 3rd XV: 13
Newcastle University 3rd XV: 22

Having scored 170 points and conceded only 11 in four games running up to the final against Warwick University, the mood in the camp was one of supreme confidence.

From the kick-off the pattern of the game was set with Newcastle's rampaging forwards knocking their smaller and less able opponents clean away. Early pressure was soon turned into points as, from a back row move, James Lloyd-Townsend smashed through three tackles to crash over.

The next 25 minutes saw Newcastle camped in Warwick's half, only for the blues to squander many of their chances – although the referee must be apportioned part of the blame for some appalling decisions. Some thumping tackles from Rob O'Kane, and the tried and tested centre pairing of Leaver and Ericker, saw the ball overturned time and again so that, just before the break, a second try followed.

From a five-metre scrum where Newcastle posted their intentions, it was a simple try for Dan Ling as the pack steamrollered Warwick over the line.

Having given away two kickable penalties, Newcastle turned round 10 – 6 up, scant reward for their domination.

With the wind behind them in the second half, Newcastle's formidable pack continued to surge into Warwick's 22. Some impressive kicking from Little and Clark compounded Warwick's troubles.

From a line-out, Little demonstrated his blistering acceleration to charge down a clearance kick and with quick hands he fulfilled his pre-match promise of scoring in the final. With the conversion again missed, Warwick came back with everything they had. However, more good kicking from Walker left them stumbling and wondering what had possessed this spirited set of Geordies.

Townsend again proved his strength in the tackle as, from another back row move, he stormed over for his second try, effectively ending any hope that Warwick had of rescuing the match. In the last move before no side, a loose pass gave Warwick a break-away try, which was converted, giving a final score that was unreflective of Newcastle's all round superiority.

11

Stopping the rot
Meaningful saturday rugby again

The failure of the University to field a senior side on Saturdays was certainly a major blow. It seemed to reflect a failure of the rugby authorities to appreciate the huge contribution that university sides have made, and still make, to the game. As I hope that this book illustrates, Newcastle University, together with other leading university clubs, are major forces regionally, nationally and internationally. Countless numbers of elite players have developed their playing credentials through the excellence of student set-ups. However, more than this, student clubs, and most certainly the Newcastle University Club, have unrivalled records of developing the rugby-playing potential of literally hundreds of young people.

The step from even the best schoolboy rugby to first class game is huge and for many players the transition through the student rugby has been an excellent introduction to higher things. It could well be that the professional clubs with their associated academies are an even better way of developing the potential of the best players in England, although the extent to which there is protection of the careers of players who do not make the grade is questionable. The game is, in any case, far more than the England team, and the demise of Newcastle University 1st XV Rugby on Saturdays had much wider implications. It affected the whole structure of the Newcastle Club – and other university clubs have presumably suffered in similar ways. It was not just elite players who suffered since, for a short time, no Newcastle University teams at all competed on Saturdays. Players at all levels in the game no longer had the opportunity to play, unless they joined outside clubs. Huge numbers of them found alternative ways of occupying themselves on Saturday afternoons – the game was losing countless numbers of recruits. Rugby's administrators in their efforts to revise the framework of the game have much to answer for in neglecting the universities. The most telling irony is that many of the same people, who had expressed their worries that young people were not playing rugby, had ignored the importance of the universities as a major nursery of the sport in England.

There were, of course, people within the Rugby Football Union who were as concerned as we were about the impacts of the National League structure on student rugby. An effort, in which Derek Morgan was deeply involved, was to form a National Saturday Student League but this was unsuccessful. In the end, it was an initiative from the three great rival universities in the North-east of England – Durham, Newcastle and Northumbria working in collaboration with Dave Shaw (RFU National Coaching and Youth Development Officer) and Peter Drewett (RFU National Student Development Officer) that enabled meaningful Saturday Rugby to take place again at Newcastle – although the new structure was quite different from anything that had gone before it.

Early meetings

An inaugural meeting took place at Cochrane Park in July 1997 at the invitation of the Newcastle University Club. It involved Ted Wood (Durham University), Ian Elvin (Northumbria University), Stewart Evans and Bernard Jones (Newcastle University), Dave Shaw and Peter Drewett. There was considerable enthusiasm from all of those present to set up a Saturday regional student league and there were also indications that a venture might well receive funding support from the RFU.

Peter Drewett suggested that a Rugby Union Student Liaison Officer (RUSLO) might be employed with the specific responsibility of running the league, and this was done in November 1997 with the appointment of Malcolm Stokoe.

A series of meetings then took place led primarily by Malcolm but with support from a wide number of people, including John Bates (also a RUSLO but who had taken over as Director of Rugby at Newcastle University), Paul McKinnon (Newcastle Falcons), Graham Solley (Sheffield University), Matt Carter, Mark Saltmarsh and David Southern (Youth Development Officers) and Derek Morgan (RFU). A range of different universities expressed interest in joining the league including Teesside, Sunderland, Bradford, York and the universities based in Sheffield and Leeds, although not all of them actually participated.

The North-east Student League Coordinator Malcolm Stokoe. Photo courtesy of Malcolm Stokoe

RFU support was forthcoming and two leagues were planned for the 1998/99 season: a Freshers' League and an Under 21 League. Malcolm Stokoe was able to arrange for the League's own stationery, posters, team and results sheets and fixture cards. The season was an immediate success:

- 42 matches were played involving nine different universities.
- More than 500 students took part.
- 1735 points were scored by 194 different players.

Northumbria University won the Freshers' League and Newcastle University the Under 21 League. However, success was by no means everything. Meaningful rugby, between well-turned out, well-coached and committed student teams, was once again part of the rugby scene in north-east England.

There were many other spin-off benefits including:

- Additional 'friendly' matches were arranged between some league teams.
- Floodlit matches were arranged between Durham, Northumbria and Newcastle Universities and Newcastle Falcons Under 19 Academy team.
- Ten members of Newcastle University represented Northumberland in the Under 21 County Championship.
- There were reports of strong bonding between players and good team spirit within each university.
- Individual team officials showed reliability and excellent leadership qualities.

Malcolm Stokoe himself made a number of observations in his report at the end of the first season:

End of season report from Malcolm Stokoe (RUSLO) on the North-east Initiative, involving North-east universities.

...FINAL OBSERVATIONS

Those universities, which had a RUSLO in close harmony, have shown the best results. Taking the nitty-gritty responsibilities from students and allowing them to get on with the job of contacting players makes the ultimate playing of regular matches on Saturdays a more obtainable thing.
Those universities, which have an adult member of staff or coach in charge, have been more likely to fulfil fixtures and have developed a stronger player base.

Certain universities have provided students with excellent organisational skills and reliability.

▶

▶ Many positive comments about the success of the initiative have been expressed to me both from students playing and administrators.

Many people, who are simply interested in the game of rugby, have expressed similar views through the regular articles in the local press.

Representatives of the local professional rugby clubs have stated that they have noticed a marked improvement in standards of play amongst the students.

Travel has caused some problems for some of the universities. With this in mind, we would recommend to other areas wishing to replicate our initiative that they try to involve universities in close proximity to each other. We would also recommend that only one age group (preferably Freshers) should be undertaken at first, building up on this in future years.

An administrator, who is fully committed time-wise to the job, is essential.

The venture has been a well worthwhile effort!

It was very clear to all of us that Malcolm's own contribution, not only in the first year but in each of the subsequent ones, has been immense.

Jimmy Merrett, club captain, receiving the trophy won by Newcastle Freshers in 1998/99.
It is being presented by Dave Thompson, Chairman of Newcastle Falcons.
Photo courtesy of John Bates

Newcastle University Freshers (in blue) versus the Rest of the League Select XV in 1998/99. Photo courtesy of John Bates

The spirit of the initiative was beautifully captured in an article written by Duncan Madsen in *The Journal*:

The Journal

Never mind the weather

In this age of professional rugby, it is easy to forget the grassroots of the game and the everyday trials and tribulations that can, and often do, ensue.

Rugby Union Student Liaison Officer (RUSLO) Malcolm Stokoe gets the flavour absolutely right when he describes a typical (?) Saturday in the new North East Universities Freshers' and Under 21 Leagues:

"Despite the atrocious weather we managed to get four games played last Saturday, one of which was a 'friendly'."

Newcastle University (under ▶

▶ the guidance of John Bates and John Elders) endured a four-and-a-quarter-hour journey to Sheffield Hallam. As they play at Abbeydale Park (Sheffield's ground), they had a 1.30 pm kick off, giving them a ten-minute warm-up! Both Newcastle sides won convincingly – the Under 21s 39 – 0 and the Freshers 40 – 0 – and were well looked after.

The journey back took one hour less including a Ferrybridge stop to empty the overflowing toilet!

Batesy got drenched watching the game and was kindly loaned a dry shirt by Alan George, Sheffield Hallam's coach. Talk about taking the shirt off one's back! Alan is due at Northumbria on Saturday so presumably he'll get his shirt back then.

Northumbria's Under 21s travelled to Bradford and were apparently 'awesome' – at least according to their Athletics Union President Ed Pettit – in winning 63 – 0, while Northumbria Freshers played a most enjoyable friendly with St Hild/Bede College, Durham, which they won 19 – 3.

On the debit side, Sheffield got to within 20 minutes of Teesside before a mobile phone misunderstanding saw them turn round and go home.

At least that was better then Leeds, who didn't have a mobile phone on board. Their bus arrived at Durham only to find that the pitches were unplayable. They were given a meal – very important for students – before heading back home. It is hoped to play these fixtures at later dates – after the monsoon season!

Keeping the momentum

A modified format was agreed for the second, and subsequent, seasons. There would be one league only – essentially an Under 21 league but one which was flexible to allow teams such as Leeds Medicals or some of the Durham College sides to include older players. Over the years some teams joined the League and others left it. It was agreed to allow some outside Club sides to enter Under 21 teams: Gosforth, Houghton-le-Spring, Percy Park and Sunderland have all done so at one time or another.

A Knock-out Cup Competition was organised from 1999/2000.

John Bates, Newcastle University's Director of Rugby, saw the initiative as an opportunity to develop young players and brought in a range of experienced coaches, from whom our players benefited enormously. John Elders, former England coach, was one of them, but others included Nelson Grey, Alan Robinson, Mike Doyle, John Fenn (who later became

Rowan Brown, captain of Newcastle University Freshers (and subsequently 1st XV captain) receiving the cup from Malcolm Stokoe after defeating Northumbria University Freshers in 1999/2000 at the Medicals ground. Photo courtesy of Malcolm Stokoe

Freshers' coaching staff: Nelson Grey, John Elders (former England coach) and John Bates. Photo courtesy of John Bates

Director of Rugby) and Steve Coombs (who went on to become the Club's chief coach). We also increased our participation in the League, in some seasons fielding four separate teams. Our commitment is reflected in several League and Cup successes.

Winners of the North-east England Saturday League

There were separate Freshers' and Under 21 Leagues in 1998/99

1998/99	Northumbria University Freshers Newcastle University Under 21
1999/2000	Northumbria Freshers
2000/01	Durham University 3rd XV
2001/02	Hatfield College
2002/03	Newcastle University Freshers
2003/04	Newcastle University Cheeky Ladies
2004/05	Newcastle University Freshers
2005/06	Leeds University Medicals
2006/07	Newcastle University Brumbies

Winners of the North-east England Saturday Knock-out Cup

1999/2000	Newcastle University Freshers
2000/01	Percy Park Under 21
2001/02	Percy Park Under 21
2002/03	Newcastle University Freshers
2003/04	Newcastle University Cheeky Ladies
2004/05	Newcastle University Freshers
2005/06	Newcastle Medicals Serpents
2006/07	No competition

Newcastle University Cheeky Ladies who did the double, winning both the league and cup in 2003/04. Photo courtesy of Malcolm Stokoe

Malcolm Stokoe also made an annual award to the best student administrative official.

North-east England Saturday Rugby: Best Student Award

1998/99	James Debenham	Leeds University
1999/2000	Alex Burton	Leeds University
2000/01	Ollie Barlow	Leeds University
2001/02	John Porter	Hatfield College
2002/03	Charlie Brough	St Hild/Bede College
2003/04	Chris Tuck	Queen's College, Stockton
2004/05	Owen Bebb	Leeds Medicals
2005/06	Will Littlejohns	Newcastle Univ. Cheeky Ladies
2006/07	Peter Clift George Johnson	Newcastle University St Cuthbert's College

After nine years, the composition of the League has changed several times but it has remained as strong, or even stronger, than ever. Twelve teams competed in 2006/07, and almost all of them completed the full fixture list.

The League Table for 2006/07. It is based on percentage points, with two points awarded for a win and one bonus point for fulfilling a fixture

Team	P	W	D	L	Bonus	Pts.	Percent
Newcastle University Brumbies	11	10	0	1	11	31	93.9
St Hild/Bede College	10	7	2	1	10	26	86.7
Queen's College, Stockton	10	6	1	3	10	23	76.7
St Cuthbert's College	10	6	0	4	10	22	73.3
Newcastle University Crusaders	10	6	0	4	10	22	73.3
Northumbria Univ. Freshers	11	4	1	6	10	19	57.6
Team Northumbria	10	5	0	5	7	17	56.7
Sunderland RFC Under 21	11	3	1	7	10	18	54.5
Newcastle Univ. Law Blacks	10	2	2	6	10	16	53.3
Newcastle Medicals Barbarians	10	2	3	5	8	15	50.0
Newcastle Univ. Highlanders	11	2	1	8	8	13	39.4
Houghton RFC Under 21	3	0	0	3	3	3	33.3

12

FLYING WITH THE FALCONS: 1996 – 2006

The advent of professional rugby has certainly resulted in heightened fitness and skill levels on the pitch, and improved organisation off it, creating further challenges for university clubs to keep abreast of developments. Two factors, above all else, have enabled Newcastle University to do so in this new era. First, the creation of a post of Director of Rugby. Second, the impact of Newcastle Falcons, which was established (initially as Newcastle Gosforth) in 1995, on the recruitment of players.

Director of Rugby

John Bates became our first Director of Rugby in 1998. He was one of the Rugby Union's RUSLOs (Rugby Union Student Liaison Officers) – former players who have been recruited to assist in the development of student rugby, with tasks ranging from coaching, administration, liaison with other clubs and referees, setting up websites, producing fixture cards, attending matches etc. John remained 'in post' until 2004, when John Fenn took over the position of Director. The role was then incorporated into a five-year development plan, in which it became a part-time university post. The plan was proposed by Club Captain Sam Brown, and supported by the Director of Physical Recreation and Sport, Graham Rayner, and the Club's Vice-Presidents' Association.

Under its Directors, the Club took huge steps forward in its organisation, running more smoothly and also forging closer links between the BUSA and inter-mural set-ups and Men's and Women's Rugby. Coaching, in particular, benefited, with an increased emphasis on developing the potential of Freshers when they first came to the university. The coaching set-up for BUSA teams was also broadened and strengthened, with first class input from Jon Curry, Matt Carter and specialist coaches from Newcastle Falcons, including Micky Ward (front row), Geoff Parling (second or back row forward) and Joe Shaw (back).

John Bates, the first Director of Rugby.
Photo courtesy of Glyn Davies

John Fenn, the current
Director of Rugby

Geoff Parling secures line-out ball for Newcastle Falcons despite the attentions of Martin Johnson. Geoff is one the Club's forwards' coaches. Photo courtesy of Sportsbeat Images

Joe Shaw, Newcastle Falcons utility back, shows Will Greenwood
a clean set of heels. Joe is one of the Club's backs' coaches.
Photo courtesy of Sportsbeat Images

The arrival of Newcastle Falcons

There is no doubt that the presence of premier rugby teams in north-east England had a positive influence on the intake of high quality rugby players into Newcastle University. Initially there were two clubs playing at premiership level in the north-east: Newcastle Gosforth (soon to become Newcastle Falcons) and West Hartlepool. Unfortunately, West Harlepool's success at the very highest levels was short-lived. They performed well until they were relegated from the Premier Division. Then, lack of strong financial backing, and loss of key players, resulted in a rapid fall from grace and further relegations over a series of seasons.

147

Coach Micky Ward, Falcons loose-head prop, sets himself to scrummage. Photo courtesy of Sportsbeat Images

Both West Hartlepool and Newcastle Gosforth introduced strong youth development programmes and these, together with the presence of quality clubs in the region, undoubtedly attracted good players to Newcastle. The knock-on effect was a marked improvement in our results. Over the next decade, universities such as Manchester, Hull, Sheffield, Leeds Metropolitan and Leeds, with which we had previously been on a par, were now regularly beaten, sometimes by large margins. For example, our 1st, 2nd and 3rd XVs amassed 230 points between them against Leeds Metropolitan in 1996/97, individual teams winning 72 – 13, 77 – 3 and 81 – 0 respectively. Similarly, at first team level, Leeds were beaten 28 – 7 and Nottingham were defeated 74 – 0 in 1997/98, Manchester succumbed to a margin of 58 − 0 and Hull just avoided conceding 100 points (92 − 5) in 1998/99.

Our rivals Durham and Northumbria, as well as Loughborough, were still recognised as leading university sides during this period but we now began to compete with them on a much more even basis. We even succeeded in defeating Durham by a couple of large scores (50 − 18 and 48 − 16), atoning to some extent for losses over many years.

Results of matches against our major rivals between 1996 and 2007

Season	Loughborough		Durham		Northumbria	
	RESULT	SCORE	RESULT	SCORE	RESULT	SCORE
1996/97			W	22 - 17	W	23 - 16
1997/98	W	20 - 0	W	50 - 18	W	24 - 10
1998/99	W	27 - 18	W	18 - 3	L	
1998/99	W	20 - 16			W	20 - 14
1999/2000	L		L	8 - 26		
2000/01	L	5 - 18	D	15 - 15	L	
2001/02	W	11 - 0	L	11 − 17	W	22 - 8
2001/02					W	25 - 0
2001/02					W	27 - 11
2002/03	L	6 - 17	W	32 - 15	L	11 - 14
2002/03	W	30 - 21	L	15 - 18	W	12 - 10
2002/03					L	6 - 9
2003/04			L	27 - 31		
2003/04			L	5 - 25		
2004/05	L	18 - 34	L	10 - 21	L	11 - 13
2004/05	L	5 - 27	L	3 - 18	L	
2005/06	-	-	-	-	D	3 - 3
2006/07	W	18 - 15	W	48 -16	W	23 - 14
2006/07	L	10 - 15	L	8 - 17	L	15 - 29

Fixtures against Loughborough University are closely contested.
Photo courtesy of Tom McNicholas

The euphoria of beating Durham (and at the Racecourse Ground too!) in 1996/97 after a long wait is echoed in Simon Hunt's report in *The Courier* in November 1996:

Seven Year Wait Ended
Durham 17 – 22 Newcastle

There are some Rugby matches that are still savoured many years after their occurrence.

And, for those fortunate enough to be part of, or witness last Wednesday's Durham v Newcastle clash, the memory of Newcastle beating their fiercest rivals for the first time in seven years in front of a horrified Durham crowd at the Racecourse ground will live longer than the drought that Newcastle's victory ended.

The Newcastle team, written ▶

▶ off by the Daily Telegraph in the build up, approached their task with a quiet confidence despite Durham's unbeaten BUSA record this season.

The opening minutes saw the huge Newcastle pack assert their dominance. Strong running from Malt and Emmerson posed problems for the Durham defence, and driving forward play led to the first try of the match as Knowles, showing a touch of genius, sliced through the Durham backs to put Wood over in the corner.

Newcastle kept the pressure up, leading to a series of penalties, of which unfortunately only one was converted. A lapse in concentration then allowed Durham to claw a try back from a scrum thirty yards out.

Newcastle then suffered another blow as the influential Knowles left the field through injury, although the fresher Thorpe made an impressive debut in his place.

Once again though Newcastle lost direction, and gave away a silly try from a charged down kick, to even up the score 10 − 10 at half-time.

The first ten minutes of the second half saw the team come under increased pressure from Durham who were able to score a third try, which was duly converted, putting them seven points ahead.

With backs against the wall, Newcastle were able to up their game when it really mattered, and showed true class and character.

A change in tactics saw the more powerful Newcastle pack begin to bulldoze a path through Durham's defence, with especially strong drives from Spence, Le Roux and Marston. The general-like half-back pair of Brosnan and Coddrington began to direct affairs and the relentless forward bombardment finally enabled Spence to go over for a well-deserved try.

Time was running out with Newcastle still behind, so they were forced to open up the game and, with a mere five minutes on the clock and the ball deep in Newcastle's own half, centres Walker and Thorpe showed electric hands to let Armitage break down the wing.

Armitage looked to be out-numbered when he reached the half-way line, but the ever-present Vyvyan appeared, and after a superbly timed pass from Armitage, outpaced the Durham defence to run half the length of the pitch for the winning try.

Durham tried to fight back but resolute defence soaked up the pressure and held them at bay. The whistle was finally blown and elated Newcastle supporters invaded the pitch to celebrate the momentous win.

Luke Edwards describes an equally exciting game when Northumbria were beaten at the end of a 10 match losing run. His report in *The Courier* reads:

the courier

Rugby Boys Pummel Northumbria
Newcastle University 23pts; Northumbria University 16pts

Newcastle's 1st XV secured a famous victory in last night's match played before a large crowd at Kingston Park, home of Newcastle Falcons.

Northumbria started the better scoring a penalty after just three minutes, leaving Newcastle to wonder if the losing streak would be extended.

Newcastle found it difficult early on but began to dominate both the scrum and the line-out, where Vyvyan and Le Roux were having great games.

A penalty went begging but the power of the pack let Newcastle crash over the line five minutes later to gain a narrow 5 – 3 lead.

Newcastle began to rise to the occasion, and Coddrington made no mistake with a penalty after 36 minutes to extend the lead, but Northumbria pressed forward before the break and only some desperate tackling saved the University.

Continued pressure by Northumbria after the break gave them a deserved try and the conversion put them 10 – 8 ahead.

Tempers flared with a mass brawl, and then Northumbria extended their lead with another penalty. But, winger Mike Wood turned the tide as he picked up the ball in his own half and showed an amazing turn of pace to dart down the right wing for a try.

Coddrington, kicking into the wind, missed the conversion so that the scores were tied at 13 – 13 as tension mounted. The miss looked as if it might be costly as Northumbria scored yet another penalty with time running out.

The University did not accept defeat though, with Nicholson stopped short of the line by a last ditch Northumbria tackle. However, the pack pressed forward and drove Northumbria over the line from five yards out. The referee took a long hard look at the mass of bodies before eventually awarding a try.

The missed conversion gave Northumbria some hope but their fate was finally settled when Tinkler made the game safe with a last minute try.

Inter-University Competitions: Northern Premier League

In order to avoid the mis-matches that were occurring between student clubs, BUSA re-organised its leagues on the basis of merit. Newcastle was rightly included in one of the two Premier Divisions (Northern and Southern). There were six teams only in the Division, including our rivals, Durham, Northumbria and Loughborough! Despite this fierce competition, we won the Northern Premier title in the first, 1997/98, season with a 100% record.

There was then a play-off against the Southern Premier League champions for the title of University Champions of England and Wales. Brunel University were our opponents and we received a nasty shock. The game, which was played at Leicester Tigers' ground, resulted in a heavy defeat. Luke Edwards reported in *The Courier*:

thecourier

Newcastle Swallowed Whole in the Tigers' Lair
Brunel University 48pts; Newcastle University 8pts

Newcastle's rugby dream turned into a cruel nightmare as they were destroyed by a rampant Brunel side.

The Newcastle defence was consistently sliced open by the power and pace of the West London side, whose back row was in formidable form.

Even in the scrum and line-out, where Newcastle have looked to have few rivals this season, Brunel oozed quality, providing some excellent ball for an attack with some awesome weaponry at its disposal.

Club captain Steve Novak and team captain Jimmy Cartmell were understandably dejected after the team's poor performance, but both were quick to see the positive side of things. Novak commented:

"It is embarrassing and it hurts to be beaten by this sort of score, but you have to learn from these sorts of experiences.

"Perhaps it was too easy for us in our League, we simply weren't used to being challenged in such a way."

The team's main priority must now be in reaching the BUSA final at Twickenham but it will be a test of their character to see how they bounce back from this thrashing.

The Club was again successful, winning the Northern Premier League in 1998/99, although there was a hiccup on the way – we lost the away game to Northumbria. However, this time the Club was more successful in the play-off against the Southern Premier League Champions, Imperial College. We won the final, which was held at Banbury Rugby Club.

The Courier's Sports Editor Luke Edwards was again the match reporter:

the courier

Imperial Minted by Newcastle

Imperial College 3 – 16 Newcastle

Rugby boys put Newcastle on the map and take BUSA Premier Crown

Newcastle University has impressively emulated the feats of Newcastle Falcons by clinching the BUSA English Premier trophy, taking the crown with a workmanlike 16 – 3 victory over Imperial College.

It was Imperial who started the stronger. The controversial venue, just one hour from Imperial but four hours from Newcastle, meant that they were the better supported side, and they were roared on by this highly partisan crowd.

Imperial duly took the lead after just seven minutes with a twenty-five yard penalty. Newcastle refused to panic at this early setback. The power of their forwards, which has been such a crucial factor in their victories this season, was once again evident as they hammered Imperial on to the back foot.

Indeed, it was through the power and technique of the forwards, ably marshalled by Johnny Marston and No 8 Qin Wiseman, that Newcastle scored the decisive try, after Tom May had tied the scores with a penalty. It arose after seventeen minutes when scrum-half Hall Charlton was on hand to seize on a powerful drive by the pack. He broke from five yards out to dive over the line. May nailed the conversion to give his side a 10 – 3 lead at half-time.

Imperial came back strongly after the break but once again it was Newcastle, through the boot of May, who claimed the crucial scores. He kicked the second of his vital penalties five minutes into the second half. Then, with ten minutes to go, he sent the Newcastle supporters into raptures, striking another penalty.

Imperial fought hard for the remainder of the match but some tremendously resolute defensive work saw Newcastle hold firm until no side.

BUSA Knock-out Competition

Regrettably, we under-performed in the knock-out rounds of the BUSA Competition. With the exception of 2004/05, we always qualified for the final stages but reached the semi-final only once (against Brunel in 2001/02). Overall, the results were as follows.

Season 1996/97		
First round	Cardiff	Lost

Season 1997/98		
First round	Swansea	8 – 35

Season 1998/99		
First round	Imperial College	16 – 3
Quarter-final	St Mary's College	20 – 22

Season 1999/2000		
First round	Birmingham	15 -24

Season 2000/01		
First round	Stirling	3 – 15

Season 2001/02		
First round	Glasgow Caledonia	46 – 0
Quarter-final	Exeter	17 – 16
Semi-final	Brunel	16 – 18

Season 2002/03		
First round	Heriot-Watt	20 – 13
Quarter-final	Northumbria	6 – 9

Season 2003/04		
First round	Swansea	13 – 3
Quarter-final	St Mary's College	Lost

Season 2004/05		
-	-	-

Season 2005/06		
First round	Bye	
Quarter-final	University of Wales Institute, Cardiff (UWIC)	16 – 19

Season 2006/07		
First round	Edinburgh	43 – 10
Quarter-final	University of Wales Institute, Cardiff (UWIC)	12 – 39

Even the great teams of 1997/98 and 1998/99 failed to do themselves justice in the knock-out stages. The 1997/98 team did not recover from the defeat by Brunel. It failed in this 'test of character' going down 8 – 35 to Swansea in the quarter-final.

Mark Lee, who later became Scotland's Seven-a-side captain, box kicks in an emphatic (50 – 18) victory over Durham in 1997/98. Jimmy Rule, subsequently Newcastle Falcons lock, and Simon Best, Irish international, are immediately in front of Mark.
Photo courtesy of The Journal

The following year was even more unfortunate. Once again, the 1st XV had appeared to be invincible, but let themselves down at a crucial stage in the competition. We were drawn against St Mary's College in the quarter-final but, despite winning the try count 4 – 1, lost the match. *The Courier*'s report:

thecourier

A Drop Goal with Four Minutes to Go and Newcastle Go Out

Heartbroken

Newcastle 20 – 22 St Mary's College

Newcastle failed to capture the form that has served them so well in this campaign and, when a spinning drop goal effort went through the posts with just four minutes remaining, there was a harsh lesson to learn about killing off your opponents when you've got the chance.

Newcastle scored four tries but failed to kick a single conversion or penalty goal, with kicker Tom May perhaps feeling the effects of last week's knee injury. He was doubtful right up until the kick-off.

Ultimately it was this that separated the two sides with the impressive running game of the visitors superbly supported by the clinical kicking of their fly-half.

Three times in the second half the Newcastle pack drove to within a yard of the line only for St Mary's to bring the rolling maul down illegally. Some referees might have given the penalty try that would have given the home side victory but on this occasion the man in yellow gave the visitors the benefit of the doubt.

It is a thin line between victory and defeat, and this time it was Marston's men who came off worse.

The visitors started strongly, scoring a try after just seven minutes. However, Newcastle bounced back with prop John Spence touching down after the forwards secured line-out ball and then drove forwards.

Two penalty goals by St Mary's were unanswered until Newcastle's best move of the match. A superb forward drive led to Sam Hanks receiving the ball. He passed it wide for winger Guy Beaumont to stretch his legs. He did so with devastating effect – charging through to score in the corner.

Another penalty gave St Mary's a 16 – 10 lead at half-time.

Five minutes after the break, Newcastle pack power was again evident. Tom May kicked for the corner and Marston won the ensuing line-out, with Spence again on hand to claim the try.

Newcastle became increasingly frustrated with the London side's spoiling tactics and tempers boiled over. Jamie Lawson-Brown became involved in a scuffle off the ball and Jimmy Rule was penalised for throwing a punch after interference at a line-out.

St Mary's broke from persistent Newcastle pressure to register their fourth penalty goal and move four points ahead.

Newcastle looked to have sealed victory when Qin Wiseman powered over the line, again following an impressive drive by the forwards.

Then, that dramatic drop goal sent Marston's side crashing out.

Scrum-half and Club Captain Luke Staton directs proceedings.
Photo courtesy of The Courier

There was, nevertheless, massive strength in depth in the Club in this season, with the 2nd XV and 3rd both reaching the semi-finals of their BUSA competitions. The seconds lost to Brunel and the thirds to Durham.

Another disappointment: 2001/02

A similar pattern was repeated in 2001/02. This time it was at the semi-final stage that we narrowly lost a game that was there for the taking. We had done well to beat a good Exeter University side in the quarter-final. Dan Foley reported the match in *The Courier*:

thecourier

Twickenham in Uni's Sights

Rugby team just one match away from
dream date at National Stadium.

Newcastle University 17   Exeter University 16

Twickenham is only one match away from the 1st XV after they beat Exeter in a nail-biting quarter-final at Cochrane Park.

They have won their way into the semis, having forced a win in conditions that make some hurricanes look like a sea breeze.

Incredibly the scoring was almost entirely from penalty kicks, with each side scoring a single try.

Newcastle started with the wind behind them, and Exeter soon realised that they would not be able to kick themselves out of trouble.

An attempted clearance from their 22 hung in the wind, and as Newcastle picked up the loose ball the visitors conceded a penalty in front of the posts. Rupert Neville stepped up and, on a day when there was no such thing as an easy kick, converted to make it 3 – 0.

David Haswell at fly-half continued to probe with up-and-unders, while the pack was re-cycling the ball well.

It looked like Newcastle had got a try after five minutes when a turnover gave Newcastle space to score in the corner, but the referee called play back for a knock-on.

Play was almost entirely in the Exeter half but Newcastle had a shock when an Exeter centre picked up a loose ball and broke through, but the referee judged him to be offside.

With the wind behind him, Neville elected to kick a penalty from just inside the Exeter half, and confidently converted to put Newcastle 6 – 0 ahead.

The restart saw Newcastle concede possession with a knock-on, and with an Exeter drive forward they won a penalty. Neville's opposite number, who kicked well throughout the game, made no mistake to close the gap to 6 – 3.

Newcastle came straight back, with forwards going in hard to follow well-placed kicks by Haswell. It looked as if James Beck had created a scoring chance but his pass went to ground. Another chance went begging as Tom Scott made an interception but again the final pass went to ground.

Newcastle were then made to pay for missed chances, as Exeter kicked a penalty to level the scores on 20 minutes. Exeter had the better of exchanges for the rest of the first half and only magnificent defensive play prevented further scores.

However, Newcastle came out from the second half firing on all cylinders. They won an Exeter throw into the line-out and drove them deep into their 22. Exeter were then forced to kill the ball, and Neville kicked a fine penalty into the wind to ▶

▶ restore the lead.

The match became increasingly physical and Ross Halliday, James Hyde, Andy Spinggay and Walter Scott all put in some huge tackles. While Exeter were matching the home side blow for blow, they were over-aggressive at times and lost two players to the sin-bin.

Newcastle took a more comfortable lead after 60 minutes, when David Gaule broke down the blind-side from a line-out and laid off the ball for Rory Best to score in the corner. Neville failed to convert: 14 – 6.

However, Exeter were far from finished. They really tested the Newcastle defence before their full-back came through at pace to score under the posts. The conversion went over and Newcastle were now only 14 – 13 in the lead.

With ten minutes remaining, Newcastle were pinned in their 22 before Halliday picked up a loose ball and off-loaded to Amabver Ladhar. What followed was the highlight of the match. Newcastle raced over the half-way line and, thanks to outstanding support play, passed the ball through almost the entire team before being awarded a penalty in front of the posts. Neville converted to make it 17 – 14.

The last 10 minutes were almost unbearable as Exeter surged forward, won a penalty and there was only one point it in.

Newcastle were able to hold on to a memorable victory, and relief at the final whistle was clear to see.

The semi-final was played at Worcester Warriors' ground the following week. This time, Geraldine Mole wrote *The Courier*'s match report:

the courier

End of the Line for Rugby Lads

Brunel dump Newcastle out of BUSA Cup in tense semi-final

Newcastle University 16   Brunel University 18

In a closely fought semi-final fixture, Newcastle went down to top seeds Brunel, forfeiting a trip to Twickenham.

Both sides started brightly with Newcastle forcing the first penalty and allowing Rupert Neville to give us a 3 – 0 lead.

However Brunel came back strongly creating the first try-scoring chance. From a scrum, they created a crafty switch which momentarily stunned the Newcastle defence into submission. It ended when scrum half Dave Gaule put in a crunching tackle on the Brunel winger.

This was followed by sustained Brunel pressure which ▶

160

▶ Newcastle managed to contain impressively, especially from the ever-committed Julian Coultas in the tackle.

Unfortunately a knock-on, followed by an infringement in Newcastle's 22 handed Brunel a penalty and the perfect opportunity to level the scores at 3 – 3.

Newcastle began to utilise their forwards, making substantial ground through a series of rolling mauls. Then, taking the ball wide out, Sandy Mitchell made a promising run up the right flank only to be tackled into touch by a tight Brunel defence.

With both sides containing strong offensive moves it was impossible to favour one side over the other, until the last few minutes of the first half. Then, the Brunel backs managed to ship the ball out wide quickly, stretching the Newcastle defence to the point where they were unable to reach the last man in the move. This allowed Brunel to run in the first try and take an 8 – 3 lead as the half ended.

Newcastle started the second half in positive spirit, applying all the early pressure with storming runs through the heart of the Brunel defence by Walter Scott. Amarveer Ladhar was also a major influence in the Newcastle backs, constantly threatening the Brunel back line.

Another well taken line-out put the forwards in a great position to drive over the line but, with the referee unsighted, Newcastle were awarded a five-metre scrum. The scrummage ball was fed quickly to fly half Dave Haswell and more quick hands gave Ladhar clear space on the right flank to storm over the line.

The conversion was missed so that the scores were level, 8 – 8. However, Newcastle gained the lead five minutes later. James Beck made a break, covering half the pitch and, although he was tackled as he cut in field, a penalty was awarded to Newcastle. It was converted by Neville: 11 – 8.

Unfortunately the lead was short-lived because Newcastle conceded a penalty in their own half for not releasing the ball.

Brunel then began to test the Newcastle defence to its limit and, although our players had looked likely to contain the onslaught, continued pressure on the try line finally took its toll. Brunel sneaked over for a converted try.

The University came back immediately but, despite retaining possession, had difficulty in making ground against a resolute defence. Brunel were then caught offside but, with the strong wind affecting his kicking ability, Neville's penalty attempt rebounded off an upright.

Gaule now made his mark on the game. An impressive line-out peel saw the Brunel defence back pedalling. Gaule took his opportunity, completing a searing run over the try line. Neville's conversion was crucial to bring the sides level but the wind caught the ball in mid-flight and what appeared to be a successful kick fell just short of the posts.

Despite continual pressure by Newcastle in the closing minutes, the score remained at 16 – 18. Newcastle were out of the cup.

Chris Small commented afterwards: "We put mind and heart into this performance but

▶ unfortunately it wasn't quite enough."

Club Captain Luke Staton concluded: "When I walked into the changing room it was like someone had died, everyone was gutted.

"We have worked hard all season and, although it wasn't the fairy tale ending we had hoped for, the lads can still be proud.

"We still have quality players we can build on next season but more importantly we have built an excellent foundation as a club rather than individual teams."

13

Inter-mural Rugby: Sound Foundations

In many ways, inter-mural rugby (referred to as constituent club rugby in the past) is the backbone of the game at Newcastle University. Yet it has been the most difficult to research and write about because so little of it has been recorded in the past. It is a proud boast of the Club that, in addition to the sides that represent, and bear the name of, Newcastle University on Wednesdays and Saturdays, another dozen or so well-organised teams from various faculties, halls or other groups, take the field. Apart from strong support from Fraser Kennedy, Performance Sport Manager in the Centre

Fraser Kennedy, the driving force behind the reorganisation of inter-mural rugby

for Physical Recreation and Sport, this effort is almost entirely student-led.

An early initiative in the development of inter-mural rugby was the formation of the Eustace Percy Hall Club in the season 1961/62 when, as King's College, we were still part of Durham University. It happened because of the increasing demand to play rugby. An early season report in *The Courier* in October 1961 read:

Courier

KRC's AMBITIOUS SEASON

Season 1961-62 marks progress and expansion in the College Rugby Club. Last season, of the initial membership of well over 100 players, only 60 could be catered for regularly by the four XVs then running – a situation not only embarrassing for the club officials, but unsatisfactory for those who had to look for games with less populous clubs in the area.

This year efforts have been made to accommodate a greater playing membership. Fixtures have been arranged for two extra XVs, which will be called Eustace Percy 1st XV and 2nd XV, and will in fact be drawn from the residents of Eustace Percy Hall. They will play against teams of senior club 3rd XV and 4th XV standard.

Every player in the College is eligible to play for King's 1st XV or 2nd XV. Below that the division will be made. Non-residents of Eustace Percy Hall will play for King's 3rd or 4th XV; residents will play for Eustace Percy 1st XV or 2nd XV.

This system gives the parent King's College Club six teams, which puts us on a par in quantity as well as quality with all the leading north-east clubs. This has been achieved without descending to the standard of 5th or 6th team Rugby in the area as we now have two 3rd XVs and two 4th XVs within the Club.

The origins of other inter-mural clubs is less clear but Henderson Hall certainly existed in 1960 because *The Courier* describes a match in which they lost 6 – 17 to Eustace Percy Hall. One famous Henderson Hall player was Dick Cowman, later to play stand-off for England. It is said that he needed to be persuaded that he had the ability to go far in the game. Once convinced, he played outstandingly for the University 1st XV in the late 1960s. Eustace Percy Hall was closed in the early 1970s but, by then, there were inter-mural sides representing Castle Leazes Hall, The Faculty of Agriculture (Agrics) and Armstrong College. Armstrong College no longer existed as part of the University as such but was retained as a rugby club for people who did not qualify for any of the other constituent clubs through residency etc. It was nevertheless highly successful, sometimes fielding as many as three XVs. A Wednesday Medicals side also competed at this level.

The inter-mural clubs normally played against one another, or other student sides, such as Durham College teams, on Wednesdays and then against outside clubs on Saturdays. Their 1st XVs competed in the Northumberland County Cup Competitions at 3rd team level, and second teams at 4th team level. They often did well. Successes include:

Eustace Percy Hall

In their first season of existence Eustace Percy Hall 1st XV reached the final of the County 3rd team Cup. They beat Gosforth 2nd XV 13 – 8 in the semi-final but then lost to Northern 3rd XV in the final.

The 1st XV reached the semi-final in 1964/65, losing 3 – 21 to Northern 3rd XV.

Agrics

Agrics reached the final of the County 3rd team Cup in 1977/78, including in their team the fresher John Jeffrey, who was later to win many caps for Scotland and represent the British Lions! JJ scored a try in the 12 – 19 loss to Gosforth.

Henderson Hall

Henderson Hall 1st XV reached the final of the third team cup in 1968/69 (see below).

They then went on to win the Cup in the following season 1969/70.

Henderson 1st and 2nd XV both reached the semi-finals of their respective Cup competitions in 1972/73. The firsts lost 8 – 39 to DHSS 1st XV and the seconds went down 6 – 20 to Blyth 1st XV.

Armstrong College

The most glorious of all cup ties was surely the final of the County third team cup in 1968/69 when Armstrong beat Henderson. An informal account of this match was given by Mike Mattock in the *NURFC Vice-Presidents' Newsletter* in January 1983:

Armstrong – Junior Cup Winners 1969

1969 was the year when Armstrong met Henderson Hall in the final of the Northumberland Junior Cup at the County Ground. After an extremely hard close-fought match, Armstrong emerged as well-deserved victors.

Subsequent winners of the cup have often queried the dents in it. The truth may now be revealed. These occurred during the 7-a-side contest held at the top of Northumberland Street at 2.30 am after the post-match dinner. Having no suitable ball at hand, it was decided that the Cup should be used instead. Unfortunately by then, passing and catching were not up to the standard of the previous afternoon.

Reorganisation

Although outside clubs undoubtedly enjoyed fixtures against student teams, the downside of inter-mural rugby was that we sometimes let our opponents down. Cancellations were forgivable when they were made several days beforehand because opponents could often pick up alternative fixtures. Unfortunately, they sometimes occurred at the last minute, usually involving away games when there were counter attractions such as televised international matches. They 'happened' as teams congregated in the Students' Union before traveling to away games. Captains became gradually aware that they would be unable to field a team and opponents were not told of the situation until just before kick-off. Occasionally the message did not get through to the opposition and referee until they were already in the changing room, preparing themselves for the match. Complaints tended to be directed either at the senior end of the club or the Centre for Physical Recreation and Sport – not at the inter-mural teams themselves!

Clearly, something had to change, as the inter-mural teams themselves recognised. The 1983 Annual General Meeting of the Club was held in February, and Tony Hay reported its decisions in *The Courier*:

All change for Rugby

SHAKE UP

Newcastle University Rugby Football Club (NURFC) decided at their AGM on Thursday to change the fixture system and team structures for both University and Constituent Clubs next season.

At present there are two NURFC teams and a host of constituent clubs also fielding more than one team each. Next season they will be arranged so that there are no constituent clubs playing on Saturdays and a limited number will play in a Newcastle/Durham league on Wednesdays.

To accommodate these changes NURFC will field five teams (1st, 2nd, 3rd and two 4th XVs) at the weekend,

and the constituents and the Medics will join with three Durham colleges in a league on Wednesdays.

The reason for this move is that the constituent clubs, who previously played against local club sides, have had difficulty in raising enough players to fulfill all of their fixture commitments. Since NURFC is held responsible for the actions of constituent clubs they have had to carry the blame, and eventually decided that the system had to be overhauled.

These changes will not affect the chances to play rugby and will ensure a better relationship with the local clubs in future.

There is no doubt that the arrangement worked in the sense that virtually no matches were cancelled because of last minute non-availability of players, and the five Saturday teams helped to foster a feeling of belonging to the whole club. This is illustrated by the pride taken, early in the next season (1983/84) when all of the Saturday sides won their matches, although by then the proposed five Saturday teams had increased to six. E W Griffiths, Sports Editor of *The Courier*, wrote – perhaps slightly over-exuberantly:

thecourier

Rugby's day of triumph

Last Saturday was one of the most glorious in the history of the University Rugby Club, and The Courier Sport takes great pleasure in presenting comprehensive coverage of the day when all six teams won. In doing so, they accumulated 137 points and conceded 23!

The First Team's win at Carlisle must stand out as the greatest achievement, but perhaps most credit must go the people who tirelessly organise the Club.

The actual results were:

1st XV	Carlisle	Won	21 -13
2nd XV (Centaurs)	Carlisle	Won	10 – 4
3rd XV (Barbarians)	Blyth	Won	37 – 0
4th XV (Trojans)	Blyth	Won	40 – 0
5th XV (Pythons)	Miners	Won	11 – 0
6th XV (Pumas)	Medics	Won	18 – 6

The lost years

A major downside of the reorganisation was that inter-mural club teams no longer entered County Cup Competitions. There is also little information remaining about the matches played in the new Wednesday League, not even the names of the winning teams. Unfortunately, this was also a period in which inter-mural rugby went through a bad patch. There were complaints that too few matches were played, due in part to the difficulty in finding referees.

Nevertheless, the structure remained intact and provided a basis for re-structuring and re-organising inter-mural rugby. It is a job that was taken over by Fraser Kennedy, then Recreation Services Manager in the Centre for Physical Recreation and Sport, in 2002. (Fraser is now Performance Sports Manager.) The first problem to address was that of providing referees. Fraser, in collaboration with the Northumberland Rugby Union Referees' Society, arranged a course for aspiring student referees. He insisted that two people from each inter-mural team attended the course so that students could provide qualified referees from among their peers.

Once the refereeing problem had been solved, it was necessary to provide meaningful competition for the participating teams. Previously, they had been organised into two divisions but only a small percentage of fixtures were fulfilled. From 2002/03 onwards, there was one league with 10 teams competing (it has since increased to 12). In addition, a knock-out cup competition and a seven-a-side tournament were organised as end-of-season events. Each of these competitions was an immediate success. Teams were well-organised, sides were immaculately turned out and matches were well-refereed. Keen team spirit was also engendered, and *The Courier* began to give excellent coverage of matches played. Not surprisingly, interest was generated in the student community as a whole and games often attracted good touchline support.

However, teams had come and gone since the 'old' days. With the exception of Armstrong, the original teams had been based on Halls of Residence or Faculties. Armstrong survived over the years, along with Agrics and Medicals, but two 'hall' teams, Henderson Hall and Castle Leazes, became defunct. Some of the teams that have replaced them, such

An inter-mural match between Agrics, probably the most successful of all inter-mural teams over the years, and Larrikins played at Close House. Photo courtesy of The Courier

as Engines (Engineers) have School or faculty allegiances but the origins (including the names) of the likes of Cheeky Ladies, Southern Fairies, Gorilla Tactics, Crayola and Larrikins are unclear.

However, the important consideration is that these teams are well-organised, tend to survive from year to year, and are a credit to rugby football at Newcastle University. The final table for the season 2006/07 is given below as an example of the league structure. It can be seen that most fixtures are completed:

	Played	Won	Drawn	Lost	Points
Gorilla Tactics	10	10	0	0	30
Cheeky Ladies	10	9	0	1	27
Agrics I	9	7	0	2	21
Larrikins	10	7	0	3	21
Armstrong	9	5	0	4	15
Titans	9	4	0	5	12
Medicals	8	4	0	4	12
Southern Fairies	9	3	1	5	10
Engines	10	3	0	7	9
Crayola	10	2	1	7	7
Mojo	10	2	0	8	6
Agrics II	10	0	0	10	0

Honours boards

Winners of the three competitions since the re-structuring of the inter-mural scheme have been:

League:

2002/03	Agrics I
2003/04	Agrics I
2004/05	Armstrong
2005/06	Agrics I
2006/07	Gorilla Tactics

Cup:

2002/03	Cheeky Ladies
2003/04	Agrics I
2004/05	Titans
2005/06	Agrics I
2006/07	Cheeky Ladies

Seven-a-side:

2002/03	Armstrong
2003/04	Cheeky Ladies
2004/05	-
2005/06	Larrikins
2006/07	Medicals

Cheeky Ladies, cup winners, applaud the opposition, after a Championship decider at Cochrane Park. Cheeky Ladies have also competed successfully in the Saturday North-east Student League and Cup. Photo courtesy of The Courier

The Director's Challenge

The Director's Challenge was another innovation, introduced in the 2003/2004 season, aimed at raising the status of inter-mural rugby and helping to promote fuller integration within the whole of the Rugby Club. The match, which has become an annual event, is between a team selected from the inter-mural clubs teams against the University 1st XV. It is now part of a wider festival of sport at Newcastle University. Fraser Kennedy was quoted in *The Courier* as saying:

> "The Inter-Mural side of University sport involves huge numbers of students. If you look at the Sports Centre's mission statement it has at its core 'Sport for all'. These trophies are an exciting, competitive way of encouraging this. The whole day will be great for players and spectators but it's also an opportunity for the BUSA teams and the inter-mural teams to learn a lot from each other. What's for sure is that before the match the banter will be severe for both sides and that's part and parcel of what the game is about."

171

The Director's Challenge games have emphasised Newcastle University's huge strength in depth in rugby. Inter-mural players relish the opportunity to pit themselves against better known opponents and, although they have usually been out-weighed up front, they have produced some good rugby and inevitably a few surprises. This was illustrated by the first match in the series which was won 10 – 5 by the BUSA side in front of several hundred spectators. Since then matches have always been well-contested and close but with the BUSA side winning.

Oli Luard secures excellent line-out possession for the 1st XV in the 2004/05 Director's Challenge match. Photo courtesy of The Courier

14

WOMEN'S RUGBY

The first call to develop a women's team at Newcastle University came on
Wednesday, 23rd January 1980. Richard Smith wrote in *The Courier*:

Courier

Give it a try...

**Come on, scrum down all women
and why not club together and
take part in a growing sport? The
latest revolutionary change in
sport is women's rugby teams!**

This is a relatively new form
of sport which has caught on in
London, and has become popular
with many colleges and universities.

The normal tranquility of
Kensington Gardens is broken every
Thursday by the shouts and cries
of women rugby players enjoying a
training session. Elderly passers-by
may stare in disbelief but gradually
the sport – traditionally one of the
most? masculine of all pastimes – is
capturing the imagination of women.
These training sessions are for
women of Imperial College and are
run under the guidance of members
of the men's first XV.

Other London colleges, as well
as Surrey and Keele Universities,
now have women's teams, and there
is a possibility that international
matches could be arranged. Now
that the original problem of lack of
opposition has been overcome,
enthusiasm is developing for the
game.

North America, particularly
Montreal, provided the foundations
for this revolution on the rugby
field. So what about Newcastle
having a try, and showing what grit
and determination can do to mould
fifteen women into a rugby team?

Progress was slow but, by March 1982, a training session had been held – and the thoughts of Sara Stewart and Debi Hind in *The Courier* were even turning to half-time entertainment!

Courier

Streaker Wanted

At last a threat to the dominance of the Men's Bar by the Men's Rugby Team... the Ladies' Rugby Team!

Don't expect the latter to sedately sip their 'G and Ts' on the 'first night of the season' event discussing the latest lipstick. They'll be in there adding a touch of class to this traditionally raucous event!

Last Thursday evening, the lower gym in the Centre for Physical Education and Sport was taken over by 30 enthusiastic but, as yet, unskilled ladies. They were under the strict supervision of John Stevens, the University Men's coach.

Training consisted of learning the basic skills of handling the ball, and being slave driven to the point of exhaustion.

Ladies' Rugby is growing in popularity throughout universities in England, including what is to become an annual event, a rugby tournament at Loughborough.

All the Newcastle team needs now is a male substitute for Erica Roe!

The team's gestation period was still slow but matches against outside opposition were played in the season 1988/89. Despite the growth of the game fixtures were difficult to come by. Most were against club sides, often involving considerable travel. The style of reporting these matches was relatively informal and brief with a strong commitment to after-match social activities, as the first short report written by "The D G King" in *The Courier* in November 1989 illustrates:

Women's Rugby 8 Durham Ladies 14

The newly ratified Women's Rugby Club lost narrowly to a well-drilled Durham team but put up an excellent second half display.

The girls conceded three early scores, but came back with good tries by Sharon and Sarah to end the game in nail-biting finish.

The Newcastle entourage then proceeded to win both the players' and spectators' boat races and drink the bar dry.

There was also a distinct element of coarse rugby in some of the early games, together with the inclusion of some characters with distinctly Mafia-like sounding names in the team. The report of the win in *The Courier* against Leicester was typical:

Courier

Glandular

Leicester 0 – 24 Newcastle

Newcastle Women's Rugby Club arrived in Leicester after a long journey to face an even longer walk to a cow pat covered field.

With a strong wind at their backs, Newcastle immediately went on the attack. Within five minutes, good team work set up the forwards who won a good ball, which was fed to Sarah Mann, the fly half, who went on a blistering blind side run to score the first try. The Newcastle forwards continued to dominate and some excellent handling by the backs allowed Dida to let her greasy hair flow behind her as she ran in for a try from forty yards out. Sarah Hudson, the No 8, then touched down twice from the base of the scrum for two push over tries.

Both tries were the result of good forwards' play with the 'likely lasses' (Purple Sal, Fiona and Ali the Ferret) in the front row playing an important part. Bullet managed to convert the last try to give Newcastle an 18 – 0 half-time lead.

The second half started with Newcastle playing against a strong wind. The forwards again dominated and, with some good running and excellent tackling in the backs, Newcastle centre Agric Emma was able to crash over for a try which Bullet again converted. A combination of exhaustion and a 'good Saturday night' saw the game through to the final whistle with no further score. Dida got the 'mammary gland of the day' award for the shortest kick ever.

Inter-university matches

University matches became the norm from 1989/90 with Newcastle competing successfully, but not outstandingly, in the Northern Group of the UAU Championship. As with the men's game, Durham, Northumbria and Loughborough were always strong and were immediately the main rivals. *The Courier's* brief report of the first fixture against Durham University reveals little of the match, but for some unexplained reason the Sports Editor's need to practise his skills in the French language. The concluding advert speaks volumes about the parlous state of the women's game at the time:

Courier

Allez Les Filles

Newcastle: 0 v. Durham University: 4

Sunday at the Medics' ground saw Newcastle Women's Rugby play a highly entertaining game against some people from Durham.

The girls in red and black lost an extremely close match by one score, with M. Le Sharpe in control (of the game, not himself) and M. Pommetonne sur le sideline.

Newcastle ran Durham all over the park, much of the play being mid-field drives. An unfortunate mistake by a Newcastle player resulted in the only try and points of the game. Otherwise defence was solid and attack was penetrating.

Notable performances were from Kicking Kate, Dividing Dida, Jinking Judy, Surreal Sal and Anxious Abi.

Wanted: Coach for forwards. No experience necessary, sense of humour essential. Suit injured player. Contact Sal via notice-board.

Rags to riches

By the time of the 1999/2000 season, the team's ambitions had grown. They were now in BUSA League Division 2 and were desperately keen to win promotion into the Premiership. But they still needed their own top-quality coach and an influx of outstanding players. Both wishes were about to be answered!

Bess Evans, a Welsh international and former Wales Under 21 coach, joined the University staff for three years and immediately took over the coaching role. Michael Walsh summed up the state of the Women's Rugby Club and the problems that Bess faced in an article in *The Courier* in November 1999:

International Welsh hooker Bess Evans gets the ball away to the backs, despite close attention of All Black forwards. As coach, Bess took the Newcastle Women's team into the BUSA Premiership and the semi-final of the knock-out competition.
Photo courtesy of the Western Mail *and* Echo

Courier

Rugby girls tackle the gender debate

The continuing success of the Newcastle Men's Rugby team has left their female counterparts with a hard act to follow. But Captain Kate Milne believes that the team can more than hold its own in a sport that is increasing in popularity.

She is quick to dismiss those who would argue that a woman's place is not on the rugby field:

"One of the attitudes that I had from one of the men's teams last year was: 'Why can't women stick to netball?'

"That sort of attitude really infuriates me because I play rugby for the same reason that any guy plays rugby – because it's a good game!"

The problem faced by the women's squad is largely due to the fact that the game continues to be regarded as a minority sport in most schools. Kate commented:

"What you've got to ▶

177

▶ remember is that most women have not been playing rugby for more than a couple of games before they start at university, so we don't really know the basics. Coaches haven't grasped the problem in previous seasons and performances have suffered as a result.

"This year Bess Evans has taken charge and is seen by all of the players to be the right person for the job. The fact that she's a woman coaching a woman's game should definitely make a difference.

"Male coaches assume that we know the basics but she's more aware of where we are starting from."

This was also a time when several outstanding players came to Newcastle University. They included Damilola Erinle, Tamara Taylor and Katie Storie, all of whom would subsequently play for England.

The first hurdle was to get promotion from Division 2 into the Premiership and this was achieved in 2000/2001. After some impressive wins in Division 2 matches, including 74 – 0 against York and 14 – 0 over Durham, the team calculated that it needed to beat Sheffield Hallam by a massive 80 points in order to win the Division (and therefore gain promotion). It did so with six points to spare. *The Courier's* report in February 2001 was now couched in more serious terms. Women's Rugby had most definitely arrived at Newcastle!

Katie Storey on the attack against Northumbria. Photo courtesy of The Courier

Damilola Erinle outpaces the opposition. Photo courtesy of The Courier

CHAMPS

In their most important match of the season, Newcastle outplayed Sheffield Hallam crushing them 86 – 0. And their remarkable points tally handed Newcastle the Division 2 title.

The University enjoyed an amazing start in the opening minute when Gill Ross took advantage of a fumbled ball to storm over for a try. Camilla Nicholson then went over for a score of her own, before the spectacular speed and side-stepping of the brilliant Dami Erinle ensured two more tries for Newcastle.

Newcastle dominated the scrums and won numerous balls in the loose.

With the Hallam defence constantly allowing gaps to open, Jane Williams managed to score two tries within three minutes by bursting through the back line.

Erinle then added two more tries to give Newcastle an incredible 42 – 0 lead at the break.

Sheffield Hallam started the second-half strongly and it was 15 minutes before Erinle added another try to the score. And then Zoe Cowell extended Newcastle's lead when she scored Newcastle's 10th try of the game.

Erinle, Sarah Martin, Sarah Western and Katie Storie completed the rout to give Newcastle an outstanding victory.

Captain Anna Pickles said:

"It was an outstanding performance by everyone.

"It is unbelievable that we started the year with only six players remaining from last year and end this year at the top of the table."

Consolidation

Following promotion, the Club then won the Northern Premiership in its first season, 2001/02, remaining undefeated throughout the campaign. Notable victories included 41 – 20 and 25 – 0 reverses for Northumbria.

Edinburgh were then defeated 28 – 17 in the quarter-final of the national knock out competition.

Loughborough were the opponents in the semi-final, which was played at Worcester RFC. Regrettably they were too strong, and the Twickenham dream vanished. Steph Stark, Women's Rugby Correspondent and team captain, wrote as follows in *The Courier*:

the courier

BUSA CUP HEARTACHE FOR RUGBY LASSES
Loughborough University 19   Newcastle University 10

The Newcastle University's team came back from the BUSA Cup semi-final yesterday, with heads held high, despite losing to Loughborough.

The girls had enjoyed an undefeated season until the clash with the Cup favourites, and were confident that a place in the final at Twickenham could be theirs.

Certainly in the first half, we looked the better team, retaining the majority of possession and winning scrums even against the head.

Loughborough were forced to play a highly defensive game as Newcastle kept them trapped in their own 22 for most of the first half.

The defence was finally broken by fly-half Dami Erinle who sneaked over the line, but this try was disallowed and it took until the last minute of the first half for Newcastle's efforts to be rewarded with a try from No 8 Tamara Taylor.

Unfortunately for Newcastle a lapse in concentration for the first 10 minutes of the second half was exploited by an angry Loughborough side who were determined that all of their 8am training sessions would not go to waste.

They scored twice in quick succession, taking the score to 12 – 5. Suddenly the tables had turned and a rejuvenated Loughborough side were looking dangerous.

Halfway through the second half they scored again, and with the score at 19 – 5 and only 15 minutes to go, a defeat for Newcastle looked inevitable.

However, Newcastle were determined to fight back. With true determination and spirit they regained control of the game, ▶

▶ and brilliant support play saw the elusive Dami Erinle finally getting the try she had been craving. This took the score to 19 – 10.

With only a few minutes to go, a fired up Newcastle took Loughborough straight back into their own 22. Cracks started to appear in the Loughborough defence and another try looked imminent. However, a ball kicked into touch with only seconds to go signalled the end of the match, the end of Newcastle's dream and the end of an amazing uninterrupted run of victories for one of the best university teams in the country.

An emotional Bess Evans, for whom this would be the last match as coach of the team, fought back tears as she told the girls how proud she was at the way they had played.

When Bess Evans left Newcastle to take up a post at Birmingham University, Graham Cooper took over the coaching. Northumbria were defeated again in the Premiership but losses to Loughborough and Leeds resulted in the team finishing runners-up in the league table.

Ironically, Newcastle were drawn against Bess Evans' 'new' team, Birmingham, in the first round of the knock-out competition. Birmingham were a strong side but were dispatched 40 – 0. Cambridge were then defeated 19 – 5 in the quarter-final.

Loughborough were again the semi-final opponents. This time the game was played at Manchester but, in other respects, history repeated itself. Heidi Swaffield reported in *The Courier*:

thecourier

Ladies have Lough time in Semi-Final

Loughborough University 32   Newcastle University 12

Before Easter the ladies had battled through the early stages of the BUSA Championship to face prestigious Loughborough in a bid for a place in the final.

Loughborough was always going to be a tough test, given that they had knocked out Newcastle from the semis the previous year.

Newcastle fought tooth and nail to attempt to lay the previous year's ghost to rest but it wasn't to be as they went down fighting at the neutral venue of Manchester Rugby Club.

Despite strong periods ▶

▶ of play by Newcastle, Loughborough's fitness and speed gave them the edge forcing Newcastle on the back foot.

The girls defended bravely with some fantastic tackling but, even after conceding some early scores, heads never went down.

Slick handling from the forwards allowed consistent re-cycling to set up some good attacking opportunities, and ever present at the rucks was mobile prop Chrissy Drewe.

Newcastle employed the forward crash ball tactic to good use, in order to keep possession away from the nippy Loughborough backs. Flankers Cat Page and Nell Gairt, and second row Leena Faulder, benefited from this strategy. Their surging runs, together with the brilliance of captain Dami Erinle, gave Loughborough a bumpy ride to Twickenham.

In the final minute of the match, Newcastle scored a team try, grounded by Heidi Swaffield, which epitomised the girls' never say die attitude.

Dami Erinle came off the pitch with a smile on her face saying:

"Despite the fact that we have missed out at Twickenham, the girls have done exceptionally well to emulate the success of last season."

Newcastle finished mid-table in the next three seasons but failed to progress beyond the quarter-final in the knock-out stages:

2003/04: Lost 5 – 34 to the College of St Mark and St John, Plymouth in the quarter-final

2004/05: Overwhelmed 0 – 60 by University of Wales Institute Cardiff (UWIC) in the quarter-final.

2005/06: Lost 0 – 31 to Edinburgh University in the first round.

Relegation: 2006/07

One of the problems in competing in the Premier League is that all of the opposition is strong. As the Men's 1st XV discovered in 2003/04, it takes only one season in which the team is below par and it is relegated. Unfortunately, the Women's 1st XV suffered this fate in 2006/07. Apart from a good win (32 – 10) over Manchester and a draw (5 – 5) against Loughborough, who were Premier League North champions and knock-out Championship runners-up, all league matches were lost. According to *The Courier's* report the Loughborough match could well have been won:

thecourier

Newcastle 5   Loughborough 5

Newcastle kicked off against Loughborough on a cold and windy day, but their aggression was not dampened by the weather.

They began strongly, driving Loughborough off the ball in scrums, and putting them under intense pressure whenever they had possession.

Though possession changed hands several times, Newcastle remained camped in Loughborough's half for long periods of the match, mainly due to Newcastle forcing several errors. Loughborough replied though and Newcastle had to work hard to prevent them from scoring.

After 20 minutes, a break by full back Zoe Williams was halted, only for Loughborough to gain possession, work the ball through their backs and score.

Newcastle came back fighting and won several penalties for Loughborough infringements. Unfortunately, they were unable to turn possession into points and the half ended with the team 0 – 5 down.

Again on the re-start, Newcastle took the game to Loughborough and after 10 minutes drove a maul to within inches of the Loughborough line. They recycled the ball, and moved it out to the wing, where Mimi Akighir dived over for a well deserved try.

Newcastle now played some fantastic rugby, putting their bodies on the line in tackles, and supporting one another well. With this rock solid defence, Loughborough were unable to cross the line again. Newcastle, on the other hand, were unlucky not to go into the lead, creating several opportunities.

Loughborough were awarded a penalty in the dying minutes but the kick went astray, leaving the final score 5 – 5.

This is the first time that Loughborough have not taken all three points from a game this season, so the result is a massive boost for Newcastle. Captain Gemma Smith was extremely happy, commenting on her pride in the team.

It is unfortunate that this standard of play was not maintained in other matches, and the team finished bottom of the final league table.

Women's Premier North in 2006/07

	P	W	D	L	Pts
Loughborough University	10	8	1	1	25
Leeds Metropolitan University	10	8	0	2	24
Birmingham University	10	7	0	3	21
Northumbria University	10	3	0	7	9
Manchester University	10	2	0	8	6
Newcastle University	**10**	**1**	**1**	**8**	**4**

There is every confidence that they will also emulate the Men's 1st XV performance and bounce back into the Premiership next season, especially under the guidance of their new coach, former Newcastle University player and English international Tamara Taylor.

However, the bonus for the season, to some extent countering the disappointing performance of the senior side, was that the newly formed 2nd XV performed well in the Northern Women's Conference. All matches were against other University 1st XVs but they finished in fourth place, winning half of them.

Women's Northern Conference 2B

	P	W	D	L	Walk-overs	Unplayed	Pts
Teesside University 1st XV	6	3	0	0	1	2	12
Sheffield Hallam 1st XV	6	4	0	2	0	0	12
Hull University 1st XV	6	4	0	1	0	1	12
Newcastle Univ. 2nd XV	**6**	**3**	**0**	**2**	**1**	**0**	**6**
York St John 1st XV	6	2	0	2	0	2	6
York University 1st XV	6	0	0	5	0	1	0
Sunderland Univ. 1st XV	6	0	0	4	0	2	0

International and current coach, Tamara Taylor, wins secure line-out ball for England. Photo courtesy of Tamara Taylor

15

POLITICS, SPORT AND INTERNATIONAL DIMENSIONS

The international dimension to rugby is one of the game's most attractive features but, at club level, it is one that has sadly declined over the past 20 or so years. While the Rugby World Cup goes from strength to strength, club tours are now much less common. They were once a normal feature of clubs' programmes, and they have certainly featured as some of the most enjoyable enterprises in the history of King's College / Newcastle University Rugby Club. They have also generated some exceptional controversy.

Politics and visitors from the southern hemisphere
Easily the most publicised visitors were those from two South African universities, Pretoria University and Orange Free State University, in 1968.

This was at a time when a policy of apartheid was practised in South Africa, and the two touring teams were composed entirely of white players. The rugby teams wanted to test themselves against university and club sides in Europe, as the first South African sides to tour outside Africa.

They came to play rugby – a view that was clearly expressed in a letter from the great South African Rugby guru Dr Danie H Craven (President of the South African Rugby Board). It epitomises the whole ethos of competition and camaraderie in rugby football:

> The two universities that are going to play matches against Newcastle University have very good records in this country and this fact alone should make the matches interesting ones. Both of them produce more representative players than any other club in their counties, and both of them regularly either win their county competitions or end runners-up.
>
> The type of Rugby they will play will be according to the true South African pattern, ie their forwards will be strong and will try to lay the foundation for their running backs. In other words spectators should be able to see good forward play in the set and loose pieces and good three-quarter play from good ball.
>
> We are grateful that two of our universities will have the opportunity of meeting Englishmen at home to experience for themselves why we have great respect for them and their rugby and to form friendships which can have everlasting effects on relationships between our two countries.

Many members of the public and the Students' Union held a totally different view. They felt that the tour was politically motivated, and that the political issues were more important than the sporting ones. It was argued that the matches amounted to recognition of apartheid by the University. A motion was put to the Students' Council proposing to levy a heavy fine on the Athletic Union, which had sanctioned the matches, but this was soundly defeated by 18 votes to 7, with 5 abstentions.

The next action was to set up a Student Action Committee to organise protests and to harass the South Africans when they visited the Students' Union. A spokesman for the Committee said that the demonstration would not be violent but:

Announcement of two international student matches in 1968. To some, incitement to protest against apartheid; to others, the opportunity to develop international friendships through rugby football. Photo courtesy of Dave Woodcock

We shall try to make them feel unwelcome and convince other students and spectators that the match and what it stands for is wrong.

The Courier issued a strong appeal against violence:

Rumours have been circulating that attempts may be made to scatter glass on the pitch, or some such ridiculous and dangerous measure. Such action would reflect the highest discredit on the University.

Fortunately the demonstrations were confined to nothing more than 'pitch sit-ins' and the matches were played – depending on your point of view, either non-violent protest or rugby can be said to have won the day!

Physical details of our visitors were received by the Rugby Club some time before they arrived, causing some apprehension in the Newcastle camp. Members of the Pretoria University team, in particular, were large – at least a stone heavier per man than the Newcastle team – and they were also experienced. Of the 28 playing members of the squad, five were Springbok trialists, 12 had represented Northern Transvaal and three had been members of a Gazelles team (Junior Springboks) that had toured Argentina in 1965.

It is no wonder that a *Courier* article included the following comment:

Having seen the statistics and photographs of the Pretoria team, it is understandable that members of the Rugby Club have stepped up their porridge consumption and are walking around with that "haunted" look.

The Pretoria match was played on Saturday 6th January at the County Ground in Gosforth (now an ASDA supermarket). It was a well-contested match, described in *The Journal* as follows:

THE JOURNAL

Newcastle University 3pts, Pretoria University 17pts

The best club match in the area undoubtedly was the visit of Pretoria University to meet Newcastle University at the County Ground, and though the South African Universities' champions won, Newcastle can take great heart from their display.

Manager of Pretoria, Professor D J Swiegers, said:

"It was one of the most enjoyable matches of the tour, and I would like to congratulate Newcastle on their excellent play."

It is not often that one sees all the points in any game come from tries – six were scored in this match and only one converted – but even more encouraging was the fact that three of them came from wing three-quarters.

Pity that the Newcastle defence failed at crucial moments, for all five Pretoria tries followed slack defence.

This was unfortunate for, in the main, the Newcastle tackling was deadly. The first try came after Newcastle had won a heel, but then lost the ball, and they allowed Le Roux to evade two tackles. The second saw Le Roux go through at least four pairs of hands. The third caught the back-row unawares when a pass went on the blind side. The fourth again saw Le Roux – a lively scrum-half – evade tackles. And the fifth, the try of the match, featured winger B J Meiring. He received the ball in his own "25" when a Newcastle raid broke down, and his exhilarating run, at speed yet jinking and side-stepping at the same time, spread-eagled the Newcastle defence. We are almost certain to hear more of this winger at international level.

The match against Orange Free State University was played on 31st January, by which time the protestors were better organised. They did disrupt play and Peter Hain, the future Labour Minister, was evidently one of those who gained access to the pitch.

Nevertheless, the game still went ahead. John Pargeter, writing in *The Journal* described it as follows:

THE JOURNAL

Tourists win – but leave it late

Newcastle University 6pts   University of Orange Free State 11pts.

A rather tame game livened up in the last 15 minutes to produce a spate of scoring, and give the tourists their first win of the tour.

I have not seen a rugby match played under such conditions, and do not wish to see another like it. For police had to ring the playing area to prevent anti-apartheid demonstrators running on to protest.

This probably put players of both sides off, especially when there were two delays because of "sit-down strikes" on the field, which meant that the police had to carry them off, and a howling gale which swirled round the County Ground did not help.

It was the tourists' first match with a university side, and one had the impression that their standard is about on a par with the best student sides in this country.

Newcastle, in fact, were perhaps a little unfortunate to lose, though defensive errors proved costly.

It was stalemate throughout the first half. The tourists were quickly up to harass, and Newcastle's efforts came to nothing because of dropped passes.

De Haas, the visitor's fly-half, looked their most dangerous runner, but he received little support, and Newcastle suffered for a similar reason. Goodall broke well, but no one was up with him.

The second half was more entertaining. Keen and Seymour inter-passed well to make ground, but when a pass from Dore was intercepted, the tourists should have scored. A pass by Burger was just forward.

Newcastle were under pressure, and Jansen just failed to hold a pass, then Newcastle had two good raids, and from a quickly taken short penalty, V Cadzow slipped the ball to Sykes who was over.

Almost immediately the score was reversed, when Haas broke well and Jansen took his pass to cross, Botha converting.

D P R Coetzee went on the blind side for another try, and Botha added a penalty goal, but Newcastle were by no means a spent force.

Holden and McManners swept play upfield. A line-out formed on the right, it led to a loose scrum in midfield, and the ball flashed out to Holden who dived over wide-out to make the margin more reasonable.

Visitors from Australia

Another visitor from the Southern Hemisphere, this time Sydney University, provided opposition in February 1976. They too were very strong, being among the best club sides in New South Wales. A special interest this time was their novel 'ball-up-the-jumper' penalty move. They used it for penalties that were wide out but inside the opposition's '25'. Basically, the forwards huddled together with the ball in their midst. One of them, then clasped the ball, still hidden from the opposition, hugging it to his chest. His colleagues all adopted the same posture and as they broke from the huddle, turning their backs on their opponents and forming a tight wall across the field, as they did so. Executed properly, as it was at Cochrane Park, the defending side could not see who held the ball. As the wall broke up, its players went off in all directions – with one of them (and the ball) hurtling towards the try line! Fortunately, Newcastle had been fore-warned of the tactic. They simply tackled anything that moved – ball or not – and the ball carrier was one of those that came to ground well short of the line. The referee was equally bemused by it all and did not object to the 'tackle orgy' so that the penalty came to nothing.

John Pargeter in *The Journal* probably underestimated the strength of the Sydney University side. Later in the tour, when they had soundly beaten Hartlepool Rovers, one of the strongest club sides in the north of England at that time, he wrote an article extolling their strengths and wondering how a student side could possess such a strong pack of forwards. His answer was that many of them were post-graduates. They were certainly an aggressive side.

Pargeter described the match with Newcastle University as an ill-tempered affair but, despite having a player sent off (which was an isolated incident), our view was that they gave us a lesson in hard, aggressive rugby. Nevertheless, he did acknowledge that Newcastle played well. Indeed, we felt that the game itself was one of the finest seen at Cochrane Park, and easily the best performance that season of a good Newcastle team that had not done itself justice in the UAU Championship. Pargeter's report read:

THE JOURNAL

Stormy match as tourist sent off

Newcastle University 23pts   Sydney University 15 pts.

The visit of the Australian tourists to the Northeast under the management of former Durham prop Bill Corkin, got off to a bad start yesterday.

Not only did the Sydney students lose the match, but they also had a player sent off...it's a long way to travel to suffer that fate!

The visitors gave a thoroughly ill-tempered display, much of which could have stemmed from frustration in that they could not win good ball. As a result, they never looked a good side. Slow in thought and deed, they shone only in their forward rushes. Here they had tremendous technique, binding and pushing in tremendous style.

But they had little idea how to get the ball out.......or it may have been by design. The halves were out of touch, the inside half invariably taking far too many paces, the fly-half always running into trouble.

As a result, as an attacking force they weren't in the game, which seemed wrong for Crowe in the centre, and Dennis at full-back looked aggressive and accomplished performers.

Very late in the game, and just before the unfortunate incident, they also delighted the crowd by trying one of the 'wall-type' short penalties – very much like American football when it is anyone's guess who has the ball. It did not come off, instead led to a scrum, and the sending off.

There was a melee and it seemed that Simpson, a prop, swung a boot at the head of a Newcastle player.

Earlier they had infringed the laws a tremendous number of times... surely interpretations can't be all that different down there... and this may have led also to one or two unnecessary actions which brought warnings from the referee.

On the brighter side, there was some good rugby from Newcastle. I haven't seen them play better all season. Dunn kicked superbly from fly-half, as did Clarkson from full-back, and the whole team figured in several sweeping handling movements which were halted only by good covering. Twice, in fact, Crowe brilliantly brought down Jarvis who seemed certain to score tries.

It was all Newcastle at the start. When a kick was charged down, Culshaw was there in a flash, and Clarkson, who made a splendid conversion, added a ▶

▶ penalty.

Crowe replied with one, but a typical forward burst by Broadbent opened the way for Routledge to add another try, before Crowe kicked his second penalty – 13 – 6 at half-time.

Not straight into a scrum gave Clarkson another three points, but only a fine tackle by Routledge on Crowe prevented a Sydney try.

Off-side gave Clarkson his third penalty which was followed by Crowe's third.

A late tackle allowed Newcastle to score another try, for the referee played advantage and Fincher nipped over… off went Simpson but, in injury time, Anthony forced his way over and Crowe converted.

The Sydney team took their defeat very seriously and spent a long time in the dressing room after the match. They were decidedly long-faced when they did eventually emerge but the after-match hospitality worked wonders and the Sydney party contributed fully to the dinner that evening. On returning home, the Club was also generous enough to write, not only thanking us for the match, but commenting that it was the finest game of rugby of the whole tour.

Another Australian university team visited us in January 1987, the University of New South Wales. They were less strong than their Sydney rivals and were soundly beaten. Jeff Brown's report in *The Courier* commented:

thecourier

Aussies sent packing

Newcastle University 31   New South Wales University 3

Three tries in each half saw Newcastle cruise to a comfortable victory over New South Wales tourists at Cochrane Park.

A patchwork Aussie XV had no answer to the hard-running home students, who moved the ball by hand at every opportunity despite the freezing conditions.

Weak in the tackle and showing little cohesion, the visitors were quickly on course for their fourth successive defeat of the month-long tour.

Newcastle on tour: the lighter side

The Club has had many successful tours. However, due to combinations of various factors, playing results were not as impressive as those in the rest of the season. Playing schedules were often absurdly ambitious, leading players were frequently unavailable due to the need to catch up on their studies and it was also necessary to give everyone on tour the chance to play. Consequently, most touring teams were probably of about 2nd XV standard.

In any case, the tour experience can be as important as the rugby itself. There is a tour mentality, which can overstep the mark, but at its best combines juvenile humour with harmless pranks. The four examples given below, which span a period of over 90 years, suggest that, in at least this aspect of the game, little has changed.

1908: Sedbergh. Many of the early tours were confined to this country, even northern England, and were relatively short. The first tour ever from a Newcastle-based team, was an excursion to Sedbergh School in 1908. School sides were on the fixture list in those days. Only a single match was played but, such were the problems of travel in those days, that the fixture can probably be regarded as a tour. *The Northerner*'s correspondent 'The Owl' described it as follows:

THE NORTHERNER
THE MAGAZINE OF THE DURHAM COLLEGE OF SCIENCE

RUGBY AT SEDBERGH

I strolled into Newcastle Central Station ten minutes before train time, and found half the team there, with the usual tale of somebody not being able to play at the last minute. The captain appeared looking very washed out. He had just come from the Motor Show, and hadn't been in bed for a few days, and refused to play. However, we found a substitute and allowed him to go home.

At Darlington we swanked along the platform while our saloon was shunted. We ☞

☞ had a pleasant journey to Kirby Stephen, where we climbed into a brake and set off on our 15-mile drive to Sedbergh. The countryside looked splendid with its late autumn tints; and as we drove further along the mists on the hilltops and swollen torrents on either side added to the picturesqueness of the scene. Rain threatened all day, but held off.

The first few miles exhausted the songs of the day, and older favourites had to be called in. After miles of loneliness and cold, we met two country maidens, and cheered them on their way. Suddenly a great shout went up as we came in sight of a girls' school. Vociferous exhortations on our part failed to entice them out, and we subsided.

The chances of the game were discussed. We hadn't played them for two years, and on the last occasion the School, with several future internationals in their team, had snatched a victory by better training.

As we drove into the School House, we let out our war cry. We were billeted in different houses, and were most hospitably received. After the cold drive, we fell into the good dinner trap, and, having had a most excellent meal, found that we had to play immediately.

We soon found our game, and our threes were in dazzling form, scoring regularly about every ten minutes.

After the game, we were made a great fuss of, and, finally, set off by a circuitous route to get back to our saloon at Kirby Stephen. At Tebay, we invaded the refreshment department in high spirits, and struck some of the very rottenest beer I have ever tasted. We took it out in a mild sugar fight.

At Darlington, we again had drinks of lemonade, and let loose our war cry to the astonishment of the fair Hebe. "Stunning girl" said one member of the scrum to another. "Sh' may be shtunning girl, ol' chap, but all I can shee is you and a lot of lightsh."

We discovered the Bishop on the platform, and gave him a rousing cheer. Nothing more happened till we came to Durham where we forcibly detained the ticket-collector till the train was going at about 20 miles an hour.

I got to the first lecture the next morning; how, I don't know, but all I could see was the blackboard and a lot of scriggles.

1952: Scotland. This Scottish tour with fixtures against St Andrews, the Royal Dick Veterinary College, Edinburgh and Glasgow University (all lost) began with a night in St Andrews. The party was blissfully unaware that it would be visiting the university town in the midst of a lively election for the position of rector. The Earl of Crawford and Lord Reith were two of the contenders. *King's Courier* reported:

KING'S COURIER

RUGGER TOUR IN SCOTLAND

It is, of course, always the happier impressions which stick in one's mind, and that is as true of rugger tours as it is of places and people and periods of time. If you were to ask a member of King's College RFC what he remembers most clearly of his three days in Scotland... it is doubtful whether he would mention rugby football at all.

We entered St Andrews at 8 pm on Monday, 3rd November after an uneventful coach journey and embarked at the Golf Hotel. After dinner we settled down in the bar in the company of some of the St Andrews team prepared for a fairly quiet evening. But we had overlooked one vital fact, namely that that the following day was the eve of polling day in the rectorial election. It was not long before the pack was called upon to form a tight scrum at the front door to hold off an army of supporters of the Earl of Crawford who had got wind of the presence in our midst of a couple of "Reith men".

They managed to escape by the back door, and, following them out into the street, we found a section of Lord Reith's supporters, dressed variously in scarlet gowns, ski-jackets and football kit, who were preparing to meet an attack from a large detachment of Crawfordites who, similarly attired, were advancing down the hill. Feeling we should announce our presence and declare our neutrality, we held up the proceedings for a few minutes with a lusty rendering of the "Blaydon Races". Then, gowns were discarded and battle commenced, with stirrup pumps and buckets of water playing a prominent part. Nobody quite knew who won.

The following morning the tour party tried its hand at golf:

> In the morning the perfect situation of the Golf Hotel became apparent. From the lounge, one looks across the 18th green of the Old Course, past the Royal and Ancient Clubhouse to the beach of shining sand sweeping away in the distance to the blue hills beyond the Firth of Tay.
>
> We thought we would play some golf. We lost three new balls in five holes, and decided that Scottish clubs are built a little differently from English ones, which is why they tend to produce a slice if you're not used to them.

1956: Northern England. One of the perennial problems facing any touring side is that it has to find somewhere to stay at night. As a general rule, inexpensive student-style accommodation is the answer. Hotels or guest houses are less than ideal, especially if they bring nocturnal rugby players into close contact with an unsuspecting general public. It was evident from the King's College tour to play Fleetwood, St Helens and Leeds University (again all lost) that even the notorious Blackpool landlady had difficulty in coping with the invasion. *King's Courier* reported:

KING'S COURIER

Some Rugby, Some Fun

In taking a child's loaded water pistol with me on the KCRFC tour, I started something, like so many people of recent years, that I failed to finish. Hitler committed suicide; today I lie in bed with pneumonia.

The first match, against Fleetwood, was played on a field that had obviously been the property of the War Agricultural Committee. The Fleetwood players played with the intent of replenishing the hungry soil with the blood of their opponents......

In the club house too, Fleetwood had the more impressive armour – the poor little water pistol collapsing in the face of a soda water siphon!

Nevertheless, that Monday evening every member equipped himself with a water pistol. The party then split into two camps ▶

▶ and battle broke out along Blackpool's rusty golden mile. The seeds of my pneumonia had been long sown.

Our Blackpool landlady was looking forward to meeting us, so she said, because she had had students before on holiday with their mothers. We were not with our mothers so she called a policeman in to take over the role of foster father. He was a nice gentleman, and even made a note of some of our names and addresses to write to us in the next week or two.

After the game at St Helens, we returned to Blackpool to retire for the night. Father tucked us into bed again and it was Wednesday morning, when the party was leaving, that we saw the sea for the first time. We knew that it existed though for our father, in one of his many jokes, threatened to throw us into the darn thing. When we left the landlady was busy writing to cancel reservations made by students' mothers for next summer.

1989: Rugby USA. Ian Aitchison, 1st XV captain for that season, wrote a report of the tour for *The Courier*, clearly elated by the fact that we actually won matches:

Rugby: USA '89

With the American economy running out of control, and good ol' George meddling in everybody's affairs, an intrepid party of 30 mercenaries gathered at Heathrow Airport for the flight to America in order to retake the colonies in the name of the Empire.

In the battle of Charles River, in steamy sauna conditions, with more water drunk during the game than beer the night before, the Yanks were dispatched 27 – 9.

From Boston, we marched up the Massachusetts Turnpike to Portsmouth. In a nice romp in the warm afternoon sun, Seacoast were sent into retreat, with a 28 – 0 hammering from the big guns.

Newhaven were current East Coast divisional champions and expected to kick our butts. Needless to say, they were disappointed when a rag bag stuffed them 22 – 9. ▶

▶ So it was back to the Turnpike and Worcester to complete the final leg of our conquest of New England. Suffering from tour fatigue, minor injuries, hangovers and spliff heads, we arrived to show the Yanks what we could do. To get 15 players out for the match was a hard struggle and with things close at half-time, and the 'Dirty Thirty' in danger of losing their unbeaten record, the big boys were brought on. Worcester eventually succumbed 34 – 18.

Some other notable tours

1951. King's College went on tour to play Nottingham University and Loughborough colleges. Unfortunately, the Nottingham match was cancelled due to frozen pitch but the ground at Loughborough was playable. The Colleges were strong then, as they are now under the guise of Loughborough University, and the match was lost 0 – 22.

1966. The Club, now Newcastle University, toured Lancashire. The results of three games played within four days were:

Orrell	Lost	0 – 3
Preston Grasshoppers	Lost	6 – 16
Warrington	Won	20 – 6

1970. An equally ambitious tour was made to the Midlands. Camp Hill Old Edwardians were beaten. There was then a narrow defeat at the hands of Moseley and a 'thrashing' from Coventry.

1976. An unbeaten tour to Amsterdam was organised by our President Professor Keith Runcorn – renowned world-wide as a brilliant scientist but somewhat less effective as a tour organiser. Morpeth RFC, of which Keith was also a member will vouch for this because they also made the mistake of allowing him to take charge of arrangements for a similar tour. Keith forgot about accommodation for the Morpeth party, and they arrived in Amsterdam without anywhere to stay. For the 26 of us from Newcastle, he arranged six games in six days, and included a visit to the Heineken Brewery in the itinerary! The latter event was at lunchtime before an afternoon fixture against Leiden University. The game was one of two halves: 0 – 0 at half-time, but 43 – 0 by the final whistle. The hardest game of the tour was against the Dutch club champions Hilversum, under floodlights. They were keen to prove themselves against British opposition and we did well to win 8 – 0.

1977. A squad of 30 players led by Dougie Currie, that season's captain, played 10 games in 21 days in the United States – Dougie had been advised by Keith Runcorn! Only one match was lost:

New York RFC	Won	10 – 6
Westchester RFC	Won	18 – 7
West Point Military Academy RFC	Won	20 – 4
Yale University	Lost	4 – 6
University of Rhode Island	Won	26 – 4
University of Pennsylvania	Won	43 – 8
University of Maryland	Won	21 – 10
Sud-Americano RFC	Won	7 – 6
Columbia University	Won	15 – 4
St John's University	Won	16 – 0

1978. Paris and South-west France. A party led by captain Mike Dudley played two matches in Paris, against sides from Stade Francais and Paris University Club, before going on to Toulouse. Matches were played against Castelnaudary, a Mirepoix Select XV, the University of Paul Sabatier and Toulouse University Club. The only defeat was to the University of Paul Sabatier. The hero of the tour was coach driver Arthur who somehow managed to take 17 hours to drive us from Paris to Toulouse. However, Stewart Evans ran him close by refereeing a fight between two French village sides, Mirepoix and Serignon, in the first round of the French

National Championship. The appointed referee had had the good sense not to turn up. The game was abandoned after 30 minutes, that is after about 20 minutes of rugby, and we eventually discovered that both teams were eliminated from the Championship.

1991. A pre-season tour was arranged to Sicily to take part in a competition with three other teams: Durham University, the Public School Wanderers and a local Sicilian club, Zagara. We were beaten by the two British teams but emerged winners against Zagara.

The Dubai experience

A sevens squad was invited to compete in the International Invitation Tournament in the Dubai Sevens in 2005. Despite the unfamiliar names of teams competing, the opposition was extremely strong. It included England's Second 7, the Saxons, although they were not in the same pool as ourselves.

There were 12 players in our squad and a party of about 2 – 3 times that number of parents supporting them.

The first series of matches was played in four pools on Day 1 of the Competition. Play was continuous so that some games took place in the middle of the day when the temperature was in the high 30s. Newcastle finished third in their pool after the following results:

Marauders	Lost	0 – 26
Kooga Whalers	Lost	0 – 24
Solo Dubai	Won	54 – 0

We then progressed to the knock-out stage of the Plate Competition:

In the quarter-final, played on Day 2, Barrelhouse Yobs were beaten 12 – 0.

In the semi-final, played on Day 3, we lost to the Russian National team 10 – 22.

However, there was an irony because the Russians were subsequently disqualified, leaving us as runners-up in the Plate.

Above: Newcastle University in the process of defeating Barrelhouse Yobs in the quarter-final of the International Invitation Tournament at the Dubai Sevens. Photo courtesy of Anthony Mellalieu

Below: A match in progress in the Dubai Stadium. The stands are temporary ones, constructed from scaffolding, and are dismantled after the event. They can accommodate 30,000 spectators. Photo courtesy of Anthony Mellalieu

16

NEWCASTLE UNITED

Sowing the seeds of a Newcastle team

The success of Newcastle Falcons in promoting rugby as a professional sport in North-east England has been remarkable by any standards. Newcastle has always been one of the greatest soccer strongholds in the country – support for Newcastle United Football Club is tremendous, irrespective it seems of the playing results! Indeed, until the advent of the Falcons, rugby had always been an alien sport to most Geordies as the following quotation from 'Argus Notes' in *The Newcastle Chronicle*, more than a century ago, illustrates:

The Newcastle Chronicle

NOT FOOTBALL

The unacquainted with the Rugby code have very original notions about the game, and an instance of this I may quote from a conversation of some youths who were admiring an illustration of the passing game on a packet of cigarettes in a shop window the other day:

"Geordy lyokheor at this footbaal match."

"That's not footbaal ye feul, that's Rugby!"

"Wey that's footbaal, isn't it"

"Nowt liket. Ye see when a chap has the baal, another chap can hoy him doon."

"Aye?"

"That's not aal either 'cos when a chaps doon an' winnit get up, ye can kick him till he drops the baal."

"Very rough like. What's the referee dee?"

"Oh nowt. He just blaase the whistle."

Now, Newcastle Falcons have excellent facilities and a crowd support base of about ten thousand – still small by comparison with soccer standards but immeasurably different from what had preceded it. In the past, local senior club games attracted small crowds, except perhaps local 'derbies' and County cup finals, although County games could attract several thousand spectators.

While the professional game has its roots in amateur Rugby Union, there are many respects in which the two run now in parallel with one another. In some ways, university clubs bridge the gap between them. This is due to strong support from students for the Falcons' player development programme. Many players have progressed from Newcastle, Durham and Northumbria universities through the Falcons system to the highest levels in the game.

In the beginning

However, Falcons did not arrive at Newcastle in a vacuum: the vision of Newcastle team had been voiced several times in the past. There had been a slow, but progressive development towards the professional era for more than 50 years. It is reported in the *Early History of Northumberland Rugby Football Union* that on 26 August 1947:

> Discussions were held of the best method to put Northumberland and Durham back on the rugby map. This is a popular topic of discussion in northern rugby circles and there is greater support given to the suggestion of a town team.
>
> It is argued that, if the north-east is to venture forth to challenge prominent national clubs, it must do so successfully. Heavy defeats would be disastrous to the cause.
>
> A Newcastle XV, it is felt, would provide a fair match for the majority of the better known British sides, it would attract the stronger city teams throughout the country and, perhaps the most important factor, it would appeal to the public.

There was a natural move towards professionalism over the next decades as clubs became better organised, prepared themselves much more seriously for matches and provided better coaching and training facilities. It became increasingly evident from the 1970s onwards that there were too many teams that considered themselves 'first class' and that the best players were spread too thinly between them. This was believed to be a particularly severe problem in the North-east. Clubs in the region were simply not in the same class as the likes of Leicester, Northampton, Coventry, Bristol and Harlequins, where outstanding talent was tending to accumulate. One consequence was that some gifted north-easterners were drifting south to join these clubs, and give themselves better chances of gaining international recognition.

Not surprisingly, the minds of northern club officials and commentators of the game returned repeatedly to considering ways in which the strength of rugby in North-east England could achieve national recognition. John Pargeter's was one of the loudest voices to further the vision of a 'Newcastle' team. The notion of bringing the best talent in the region together to challenge the best clubs in England was simple enough but it was still a long way from reaching fruition. Writing in *The Journal* in February 1970, Pargeter expressed the following views:

THE JOURNAL

Combined team is the only solution

The more one sees of club rugby on Tyneside, the more one is driven to the conclusion that a Newcastle XV is the only solution.

The laws of the game, as they are now framed, should be producing open attacking rugby, but this can only be achieved if all the players have the ability. It is no good if only half the side is sufficiently capable.

At the weekend a Northern side, which has disappointed most of the season, lost 3 – 12 to a below strength Hull and East Riding side, and Northern only managed a fortuitous try.

Across the Great North Road at Gosforth's ground, the home team struggled to beat Wilmslow by 9 – 3, all of their points coming from kicks.

At both matches, the attendances were poor. True, there has been a surfeit of top-class rugby on the

television screen this season with the South African tour, followed by the Home Internationals, but good rugby will always draw a crowd.

There is a great deal going on behind the scenes at national level at the moment to form a league, and if the North-East, especially Tyneside, does not wish to be left out in the cold, something has got to be done.

A combined Newcastle side would be almost the strength of a county team. It would certainly be sufficiently strong to take on any club side in the country.

The situation calls for a cool discussion. If something is not done shortly, simple economics may force the issue, for it is debatable how long both Northern and Gosforth can struggle along under existing circumstances – playing-wise or cash-wise as the modern expressions go.

It was a debate that would continue for more than a decade and a half, although, to some extent, the problem seemed to be solving itself with the gravitation of players to the better clubs – in the case of Newcastle and Northumberland, to Gosforth. John Pargeter commented in *The Journal*:

THE JOURNAL

Gosforth corner the star market

Gosforth seem to be attracting star rugby players like moths to a light... and one or two voices have been raised in protest.

So typical of rugby, however, no one is prepared to be quoted in criticism, simply asking me to fire the bullets.

Said a member of one club: "It's been known for years that Gosforth have poached players, but what do they want to do... put all the eggs in one basket?"

And another: "If this trend goes on, there will be only one club left. The others will just be feeding players into Gosforth."

Yet another: "It is not encouraging to us to train a player to a certain standard and then lose him to Gosforth."

I can't go along with these criticisms, however, for it is many years since I first wrote about the possibility of a Newcastle side. It is more topical than ever in view of Gosforth's growing prowess... but is it too late?

Getting down to brass tacks, it boils down to the fact that other clubs are jealous. Yet they have had the same opportunity. While they have been quite happy to plod along, Gosforth have looked ahead....and far ahead. From scratch they have built up a tremendous organisation and they now have a reputation throughout the country.

I still think that it would be a good idea to form a Newcastle side... simply change the name of Gosforth if you like to Newcastle. It would have a greater impact, and then players would be freer to join.

To watch that type of rugby the crowds would soon grow. Other clubs would barely be affected. At least they would all be on a par.

Of course, clubs did not like to lose their best players and, as John Pargeter found, accusations of poaching were rife. It was difficult to know to what extent they were true and even more difficult to prevent 'unofficial' approaches to players. However, it was not a new problem and, according to *Rugby Notes* published in the *Newcastle Chronicle* in October 1894, Hartlepool Rovers had a novel solution to the problem as far back as the nineteenth century:

The Newcastle Chronicle

Poaching by a Northumberland club sounds strange and improbable. It has nevertheless been attempted. The individual who acted as an agent in this matter showed shockingly poor judgment in the players he required. But he is no diplomat, and had a near escape from a dip in the docks at Hartlepool.

This adventurer, who was plucky enough to go after two of the best men in the Rovers team, was lucky to get off so easily.

I understand that nothing further will be done in the matter, and can quite believe that after the excitement caused in the Hartlepools no one with any regard for his future will try the game on there again.

However, poaching was not the cause of Gosforth's success. The Club became so much better than its rivals that, as Pargeter comments, better players naturally wanted to play for it. Gosforth's golden era was from the mid-1970s until the early 1980s. For a time, the Club was arguably the strongest in England. It literally teemed with internationals, including Roger Uttley, Duncan Madsen, Jim Pollock, Malcolm Young, David Robinson and Colin White. In 1976, Gosforth beat Rosslyn Park 23 – 14 in the Twickenham final of the Powergen Cup (the fore-runner of the John Player Cup) and, in the following year repeated the success, defeating Waterloo 27 – 14.

Three former Newcastle University players who have used the 'Newcastle experience'
to the full and have become well-known names in premiership rugby:

Top left: *Tom May, who has represented England A in action in a Heineken Cup match*
against Perpignan. Photo courtesy of Sportsbeat Images

Top right: *Hugh Vyvyan, who was capped for England against Canada and captained an*
England XV against the Barbarians. Photo courtesy of Sportsbeat Images

Bottom: *Hall Charlton, who has been replacement scrum-half for England, gets the ball*
away in a Heineken Cup match against Stade Francais. Photo courtesy of Sportsbeat
Images

Good things never last

Gosforth remained outstandingly strong in terms of rugby in North-east England in the mid-1980s but their heyday had passed. Players were no longer automatically electing to join the Club and results against leading British clubs were suffering. Following a 6 – 21 defeat at the hands of London Scottish, and the resignation of the Club's hooker, an article by Duncan Madsen appeared in the *Evening Chronicle* on Tuesday, 14 January 1986:

EVENING Chronicle

Testing time for Gosforth

...before anyone should wish to bring personalities into it, they should take note of the list of players who have been dropped in the last two years and who have promptly left the club.

Two conclusions are inescapable. Either there is a communication and man-management problem between the selection committee and players or the Gosforth first team players have become so elitist that no one wants to play for any other team in the club.

On the subject of elitism, it should be remembered that Gosforth, like any other club, is much bigger than the first team.

When they were enjoying unparalleled success in the 1970s, the Gosforth team was very approachable by all club members and were certainly not a team within a club.

If this feeling does not now exist, the club captain should be telling his men a few home truths. One is that no rugby club is an island, in that it must exist with the clubs within the area. Northumberland County Rugby is taken very seriously by players and members of other clubs. They were very hurt by the response of certain players who refused to play for the County in the match against Cumbria.

Gosforth and the rest of Northumberland Rugby should be mutually compatible and beneficial but, once such bonds are broken, it is both who will suffer in the short and long terms.

The last paragraph in particular seemed to offer wise and, as it turned out, prophetic advice!

Shooting themselves in the foot

An exciting development towards a 'Newcastle' side was initiated by the Gosforth club at the beginning of the 1986/87 season. The prime mover was Gosforth's Vice-President David Campbell. He wrote to local clubs explaining his vision of an area team and inviting club representatives to a meeting to discuss the possibility. The area team would be based on Gosforth which was now planning to sell its existing ground on the Great North Road and relocate itself at Kingston Park, about three miles away. The intention was to pool regional resources in order to guarantee first class club rugby in the region. It was argued that there were too many clubs competing with one another in the area and that the consequent dilution of playing resources meant that we lacked a genuine first class club. There could also be financial advantages since the costs of playing at the top, with fixtures across the country, would be considerable. It was inconceivable that more than one club in the region could afford to compete at this level but a first class side might do so by attracting sponsorship and income from gate money.

There was substantial support for the proposal at the first meeting on Tuesday 25th November 1986, particularly from players. Ronnie Tait of Berwick Rugby Club summed up their feelings and, in doing so, expressed views that were fully in accord with those of our own club. Duncan Madsen reported it as follows in the *Evening Chronicle*:

> At Berwick we have always supported any player who has moved on to better himself and the likes of Ian Ramage, Ian Roughead and Andy Hindhaugh moved on with our blessing.
>
> As far as I am concerned a scheme such as has been outlined here can do nothing but benefit the whole of North-East Rugby.

Our own contribution to the meeting was:

Stewart Evans of Newcastle University said that he was

in favour of further talks, a sentiment backed by Seghill's John Atherton and others.

It was agreed that the club representatives would return to their clubs with the proposals produced by Gosforth for discussion.

However, in spite of enthusiastic support from the press, the proposal was doomed. Tynedale had not attended the meeting, Morpeth were undecided and then Northern announced publicly in a letter published in the *Evening Chronicle* and circulated to all clubs that they were opposed to it. The area talks fizzled out inconclusively; perhaps, as Duncan Madsen had pointed out, Gosforth had paid insufficient attention to its relationships with other clubs in the region.

The prospect of a Newcastle side emerged again in the following year with the proposal that Gosforth and Northern might merge, pooling their financial and playing resources. This suggestion was again supported by the press but it too was probably always a non-starter – it certainly never happened!

The latest chapter

Nevertheless an area side was eventually formed and Gosforth was the basis. The developments are elegantly summarised on the Newcastle Falcons website (www.newcastle-falcons.co.uk):

About us

Despite some comparatively lean years for Gosforth, a major transition was on its way. In 1989, they decided to sell their North Road Ground for £1.7million to a housing developer, and set about purchasing the Newcastle Chronicle and Journal sports ground at Kingston Park for only £55,000.

The Club spent a season playing at Percy Park RFC while this work was completed, and in 1990 they moved into their new home, also under a new name – Newcastle Gosforth.

Up-and-down results and financial problems beset the Club, and in September 1995, it was to undergo another major change, when ▶

▶ Newcastle United soccer chairman Sir John Hall realised his long-held dream of establishing a Newcastle Sporting Club, encompassing Rugby Union.

The recent change to legalising professionalism in the game had facilitated the move, and with Newcastle Gosforth's fortunes on and off the field diminishing somewhat, Hall's involvement could hardly have come at a better time.

Hall's new Sporting Club held 76 per cent of the shares in the Club, while the other 24 per cent was held by the Newcastle Gosforth members. To this day, the '24 per centers' as they are known, are still involved with the Club, and provide valuable support.

Having secured the Club's future, Hall then set about instituting one of the biggest makeovers in sporting history, recruiting Wasps and England fly half Rob Andrew as Director of Rugby and star player, as well as other high profile signings. Dean Ryan and Steve Bates were enlisted as key coaching and playing figures, while the likes of All Black Inga Tuigamala, Scotland stars Gary Armstrong and Doddie Weir, and England's Tony Underwood soon followed.

The 1996/97 season saw the first under the current name of Newcastle Falcons, and the Club also changed its colours to black and white. That year saw the team rise through the second tier of English club Rugby and clinch promotion to the Premiership, scoring masses of points on the way.

The 1997/98 season was then to go down as arguably the biggest in the Club's history, as the all-star squad sensationally went on to lift the Allied Dunbar Premiership trophy in the first season back in the top flight.

Saracens pushed them all the way, but a sun-backed afternoon as The Stoop saw the north-easterners gain the necessary win against Harlequins that they needed to stave off the Sarries challenge. The feat was then followed straightaway with a dramatic win over a World XV in the Sanyo Cup at Twickenham.

Rugby politics denied the Falcons a chance to have a crack at the Heineken Cup the season after, as English clubs embargoed the competition for a year, and it was 1999 before the club next had the chance to win a trophy – sadly, a Twickenham defeat to London Wasps in the Tetley's Bitter Cup final.

It was that year, however, that the latest chapter in the Club took flight, when current Chairman David Thompson bought out Sir John ▶

▶ Hall's Sporting Club shareholding. Thompson, a businessman but also a keen local rugby man, kept faith with the coaching team, and made sure that professional rugby survived in the north-east.

Indeed, it was with his backing that the Club reached the 2001 Tetley's Bitter Cup final, where a last minute try from Dave Walder secured a dramatic late win over NEC Harlequins.

The team then repeated this success in 2004, when more than 50 bus-loads of supporters made the trip down the M1 to Twickenham to see a thrilling Powergen Cup final victory over Sale Sharks, with Phil Dowson pouncing for the winning try towards the end of the second half.

So, after more than a century-and-a-quarter of existence, it is clear that the history of Newcastle Falcons – under whichever name and at whichever ground – has been one of great persistence and resilience, under-pinned by the dedication of those charged with its upkeep, and its loyal growing support base.

Rob Andrew addresses a press conference describing plans for the new Newcastle Gosforth Club (later to become Newcastle Falcons). He is supported by Sir John Hall, Tony Underwood and Doddie Weir. Photo courtesy of The Journal

The Falcons had the advantage of coming to Newcastle with a clean sheet – they had no 'hang-ups' with other clubs in the region. By no means everyone was happy to see the famous name of Gosforth disappear, together with much of what the Club had stood for, but the Falcons' success has been extraordinary. Local support has been amazing, presenting an interesting mix of ardent followers, comprising present and former rugby players as well as local converts who have probably never played the game.

The Falcons also came to the North-east with a vision of how the game should develop here and, although their initial successes were due to the influx of world class players brought in from outside, they paid special attention to forming good community relationships, including close links with schools and universities, and an excellent youth development programme. Careful consideration was also given to the longer-term developments of players and the acceptance that only some promising players would 'make the grade' sufficiently well to make a living out of the game. James Jordan reported comments from Rob Andrew in an interview for *The Courier* on 7 March 1996:

> ...he stressed that education must come first and the club would not want any prospective pro to give up his studies simply to play. "It would be dangerous," he argued, "not to have anything to fall back on in case of injury or not getting another contract. The University and Club must complement each other. A successful Newcastle would only enhance the reputation of the University as a place to which young sportspeople should come."

The set-up has meant that outstanding players, including Rory and Simon Best (Ireland), Hugh Vyvyan, Tom May and Hall Charlton (all England 'A' players) could get the best of all worlds in the 'Newcastle experience'. They could come to a leading provincial university to study for their chosen degrees and acquire first class qualification but, at the same time, play good quality student rugby and then, through the Falcons, develop their full potential as rugby players. The tradition now continues under John Fletcher, who took over as Director of Rugby from Rob Andrew in 2006. The most successful student players continue to find their way into the Falcons set-up.

*The Best brothers. Two of the former Newcastle University players who have gone on to represent Ireland. **Above:** Prop Simon Best in action against Italy. Simon captained the Irish team on tour in Argentina **Below:** Hooker Rory Best scores a try against Wales Photographs courtesy of Inpho Photography*

17

BOYS BEHAVING BADLY

The social side of rugby has always given the sport a unique, and not always wholly acceptable, image. Rugby players are by repute great beer drinkers and revel in after-match fun, including ingenious drinking games which have complex rules and series of (drinking) penalties that only the 'chairman' (and certainly not the opposition) can understand. Games are interspersed with bouts of singing, which is often untuneful but never lacking in vigour. The words of bawdy songs are passed from generation to generation and, once armed with a repertoire of songs, so does the player's confidence to participate. One year's timid Fresher may be found three years later orchestrating the evening's entertainment!

This revelry has probably always been the case. Certainly, the high spirits were evident in the glory days of the late 1960s, when *The Courier's* correspondents were keen to add postscripts to reports, describing after-match activities. Following the match against Gateshead Fell in March 1968:

> ...and it took inspiring captain Woodcock to break the deadlock and show the way to victory – and the bar – where Keen beat Seymour in a straight contest. (Next week: Seymour v. Keen rematch; University v. Manchester).

After a UAU match for both the First XV and Centaurs at Hull in October 1968:

> During the drinking after the game, and the bus journey home, certain people were careless enough to lose several things. Hull Union lost its sombre dignity; W A Clark lost his beard; and Centaurs lost G Fawcett. We were also treated to the sight of a first team player eating raw fish. I always wondered what one had to do to become a first team player.

Following a victory over Sheffield University in a UAU match in February 1970:

> Several friendships were formed or renewed: Forbes with snow-covered pitches; Moriarity with 'mild'; Kerss with soda; Cowman with lager; Woodcock with sobriety; and Sheffield University with real rugby teams. An attempt to eject us from the Sheffield Union at 8 pm failed miserably because they couldn't tell us from the rowdy Sheffield students.

Finally, a short play, written after a victory over Carlisle:

A POT OF HONEY...
A POT OF HONEY
Sour Grapes – A Tradgedie.

A DRAMATIC PRESENTATIONE FOR THE EDIFICATION
AND DELYTE OF THE PUBLIKE, IN ONE ACTE.

Enter smooth-talking rugby player (perm any one from 15) and gorgeous blonde.

SMOOTHIE – *"Here is your half of mild, dear. Now... what is your connection with Carlisle RFC?"*

BLONDE SMILING – *"My husband plays tight head prop."*

ENTER STAGE RIGHT: *Person of enormous proportions with no neck.*

EXIT STAGE LEFT: *One rugby player whimpering hysterically.*

Applause... and CURTAINS.

A tad too far

Unfortunately boisterous behaviour can go too far and there have been occasions on which members of the Club have let us down. 'Initiation nights' have caused occasional problems in the past and so too Club dinners – not because of damage but because many establishments react negatively to the raucous, medieval atmosphere that rugby players can generate. Coaches on the way home have sometimes also been the focus of indiscipline. However, the Club values its image and now has its own 'Code of Conduct' to which players are expected to conform.

There have been problems in finding venues for the Club dinner in the past and these were emphasised following HRH The Queen Mother's visit to Newcastle in the 1980s. It was an honour that she was given lunch in the University Refectory, and, according to all accounts, the Refectory did The Queen Mother and the University proud.

The Refectory had also hosted the Rugby Club's annual dinners for the past three years and, in these cases too, it had performed very well. The events were perhaps boisterous but everyone, including the Refectory staff, and especially the waitresses, enjoyed the evenings – or so it seemed!

The telephone conversation between the Club Captain and the person taking reservations on behalf of the University's Catering Manager went something like this when a request was made to return to the Refectory for the fourth consecutive dinner:

> "Good morning. I shall be grateful if we could make a booking for the Rugby Club's Annual Dinner for the last Saturday in March."

> "I am sorry but we are fully booked then."

> "OK we are fairly flexible and that should not be a problem. On which Saturdays could you take a booking?"

> "I am afraid that we shall not be able to accept a booking at all from the Rugby Club this year."

> "But why not? There were no problems last year, nor in either of the years prior to that? They were successful dinners."

> "Unfortunately, an establishment that hosts the likes of the Queen Mother cannot accept the Rugby Club! Good morning."

The bare facts

Rugby players seem to have an insatiable need to take their clothes off. The explanation is unclear and undoubtedly complex – probably best left for future generations of psychologists!

The lads in training for their sponsorship deal! Photo courtesy of The Journal

However, rugby players can also be inventive and opportunistic and have, on a couple of occasions, actually made money by undressing themselves. In February 1994, members of the Club received sponsorship from Scottish & Newcastle Breweries by taking part in an advertising campaign for Newcastle Brown Ale. Miles Starforth and Simon Bird reported developments in a front page article in *The Courier*:

RUGBY BOYS REVEAL ALL IN NATIONAL
BROWN ALE POSTER CAMPAIGN

Brown Ale Ad nuts shocker for our Rugby models

Naked University rugby players are set to shock the nation by appearing starkers in a major beer advertising campaign with only bags of nuts covering their manhood, The Courier can exclusively reveal today.

Brown Ale brewers Scottish and Newcastle are to launch a massive sales push by giving away a bag of peanuts free with every bottle of Brown bought. Newcastle University's strapping players will prove cracking models by revealing everything, bar their own 'nuts'.

Boosted by the slogan "Nuts to Newcastle Brown Drinkers," the saucy campaign will hit the street in the next couple of months.

However, the campaign took some rather unexpected directions. Miles Starforth wrote a follow-up article in March 1994:

the courier

Bringing a whole new meaning to the word tackle!

Newcastle University's rugby team have not been out of the headlines since The Courier exclusively broke the story of their naked posing two weeks ago – some of them are even set to appear in a television sex guide.

No sooner had the paper come off the press than the Evening Chronicle, The Sun, Today and a host of news agencies were chasing the story.

The rugby boys were even featured alongside a top 'Page 3 girl' in one tabloid.

And now top sex expert Margi Clarke has approached the ▶

▶ team to talk about their sex lives on ITV's Good Sex Guide.

It is rumoured that the players will this time use rugby balls to protect their modesty.

The Rugby Club captain told The Courier:

"The original advert has been blown out of all proportion. Only the other day we were saying in the Union how a television company would be in touch soon – when we got home one had!

"But when half of us are future lawyers we would need a lot of persuading to appear on some sex guide."

The Good Sex Guide appeared that autumn, and some players were also featured on ITV's business programme Commercial Break. In it, Paul Stranger, Brand Manager for Scottish & Newcastle explained that the Brewery had been looking for a creative twist that would bring a smile to people's faces. He said:

> We knew we'd only be able to get students to do it and we thought that we would have to ask a few institutions before we got our volunteers.

> But the Newcastle lads were the first that we tried – and they accepted straight away!

18

THE LION ROARS: 2006 – 2007

The season 2006/07 has now been completed and, in many ways, typifies the strengths and weaknesses of the Club. Playing records have been outstanding across all of our teams. The Club entered a 4th XV in the BUSA competitions for the first time (one of a tiny number of universities to do so) and it, together with the senior three teams, performed well.

BUSA awards points on the basis of team performances in leagues and the knock-out competitions. Newcastle Rugby finished third nationally, after only Hartpury College and University of Wales Institute Cardiff (UWIC), in tallies for Men's Rugby.

Top five universities in points awarded for Men's Rugby in 2006/07

Position		Total Points
1	Hartpury College	164
2	University of Wales Institute, Cardiff (UWIC)	148
3	**Newcastle University**	**125**
4	Nottingham University	110
5	Loughborough University	100

Our close rivals, Northumbria and Durham, were awarded 94 and 84 points respectively.

So how did we amass these points?

First XV

The team competed in the Men's Premier North A, and finished second overall.

Men's Premier North A League Table 2006/07

	P	W	D	L	Pts
Northumbria University	12	10	0	2	30
Newcastle University	**12**	**8**	**0**	**4**	**24**
Loughborough University	12	7	0	5	21
Nottingham University	12	7	0	5	21
Durham University	12	6	0	6	18
Birmingham University	12	2	0	10	6
Worcester University	12	2	0	10	6

There were some excellent games of rugby, including two against our closest rivals, Durham and Northumbria. Ben Anderson and Will Bain reported the away game against Durham in *The Courier*:

Steve Coombs, Head Coach in 2006/07.
Photo courtesy of Tom McNicholas

thecourier

Durham Demolished

DURHAM 16   NEWCASTLE 48

Though perhaps not at their outstanding best, Newcastle were still impressive in their rampant 48 – 16 demolition of close rivals Durham.

Although the hosts had their chances, Newcastle were without doubt the more clinical of the two sides, running in almost a half-ton.

Newcastle took the game by the scruff of the neck early, a point-a-minute scoring rate saw them take a commanding 22 – 3 lead after the first quarter, through tries from Robbie Kalbraier, Rob Jackson and Rob Kyle.

Durham's response was futile with a lone penalty to their name. However, they got themselves back into the match with some tidy kicking, with a penalty, quickly followed by a neat drop goal from Timmy Taylor.

Spurred on by this, the home side rallied. However, a missed penalty and then a superb last ditch tackle from full-back Brian Magookin prevented the Durham winger from going under the posts for their first try. Another Newcastle penalty ensued and the team went into the interval 25 – 9 to the good.

The away side increased the tempo once again in the second half, with Rob Jackson making a fine run. Newcastle's pack then came to the fore with two tries in quick succession from rolling mauls developed from secure line-out ball, killing off any hopes that Durham may have had of getting back into the match. Tim Swinson and Ciaran McNicholas were the beneficiaries, with Anthony Mellalieu adding the conversions.

Durham threatened in fits and starts, with replacement forward Tim Walford making his presence known with several big tackles, and Taylor always looked dangerous with slick side-steps that sometimes breached Newcastle's first line of defence.

However, they lacked conviction in the final third of the pitch, and the one clear-cut chance that they did have came to a premature end as Newcastle wing Dave Warwick put in a magnificent tackle on Leroy Basey.

To their credit, Durham kept on fighting and nipped in for a consolation try. But, as was the pattern of the afternoon, just as Durham scored Newcastle came to life, with the best two tries of the game. Chris Clarke backed his speed with a mazy thirty-yard run to go in the corner. Yet, the best of all came from James Burns who left four defenders eating the dust with his galloping run, even throwing in a classy side-step to round the last man.

As the hosts trudged off, Newcastle's victory chorus rang clearly out for all to hear!

The finest performance of the season was nevertheless reserved for the away match against Northumbria. Paul Christian reported in *The Courier*:

the courier

Newcastle Rampant

NORTHUMBRIA 14 NEWCASTLE 23

A glorious night, a heroic performance, a euphoric result! In fear of running out of superlatives let's leave it at this – oh how sweet victory is!

Played at a wonderfully lit Kingston Park, the hub of rugby on Tyneside, a classy Newcastle side rose to the occasion and produced an unforgettable performance that was fit enough to grace any game.

The atmosphere was electric and added an extra level of intensity to a spectacle that was already certain to raise pulses. Both teams exploded from the starting blocks in typical derby fashion, desperate to impose themselves early. However, Newcastle's strength was evident. Good work from the line-out resulted in the first penalty of the game, which Newcastle's fly-half Anthony Mellalieu dutifully converted.

Newcastle maintained their pressure. Captain Ben Duncan led from the front with a series of inspiring tackles, while the dominance of the Newcastle forwards kept Northumbria camped deep in their own half. Another score was inevitable, and score we did. Mellalieu converted his second penalty of the game, majestically stoking the ball over from almost half way. Northumbria's spirits were noticeably flagging!

The first-half rout continued despite Mellalieu missing a third penalty attempt. Newcastle's forwards over-powered Northumbria's and forced the ball over the line after a rolling maul. The try was scored by Andy McDonald. Minutes later Chris Davison glided through our opponents' crumbling defence and forced the ball over the line to send the Northumbria side into utter despair. Mellalieu effortlessly converted both tries and the half-time scoreboard read a sweeping 20 – 0 to our boys.

Well, in short, rugby is after all a game of two halves and Northumbria certainly improved after the break. A sustained period of pressure was held off for the most part by a resilient Newcastle defence but a neat kick from Northumbria's fly-half James Ferguson was met by James Hamer for a try.

Nonetheless, despite having less possession, Newcastle still looked in control and another penalty conversion from the outstanding Mellelieu increased the lead. A late try and conversion saved little face for Northumbria. The final whistle came leaving the sweet taste of success in the mouth of head coach Steve Coombs and everyone else associated with Newcastle University.

The first round of the knock-out tournament saw an emphatic win over Edinburgh. *The Courier* summed it up as follows:

thecourier

Scotch missed

NEWCASTLE 43   EDINBURGH 10

A wet and windy afternoon at Cochrane Park played host to a Newcastle master class as the home side demolished their Scottish opponents in emphatic fashion.

Barely had the quarter hour mark passed before Newcastle were already 19 – 0 up after an explosive start that all but killed off the game as a contest.

Unfortunately, the quarter-final saw our exit, losing 12 – 39 to a powerful University of Wales Institute Cardiff (UWIC) side, hardened no doubt by their experiences in the Welsh National First Division.

Second XV

The seconds won a particularly strong Northern Conference 1A League in which, apart from Durham and Northumbria 2nd XVs, they were playing against other university 1st XVs.

Northern Conference 1A League Table 2006/07

	P	W	D	L	Walk-overs	Unplayed	Pts
Newcastle 2nd XV	14	12	1	1	0	0	37
Durham 2nd XV	14	10	0	2	2	0	36
Liverpool 1st XV	14	8	1	5	0	0	25
Northumbria 2nd XV	14	8	0	4	0	2	24
Hull 1st XV	14	6	0	7	0	1	18
Lancaster 1st XV	14	4	0	8	1	1	9
Chester 1st XV	14	1	0	13	0	0	3
Keele 1st XV	14	2	0	11	1	0	3

In the last match of the league season we had to beat Liverpool, with whom we had drawn earlier in the season, to finish ahead of Durham and win the League. *The Courier's* report of the match:

the courier

Newcastle's delight

NEWCASTLE 2ND XV 31   LIVERPOOL 1ST XV 23

Newcastle's second stream continued to fly the blue and white flag with pride as they defeated Liverpool University to win their league and become the highest placed second team in the country.

Hearts were full of fire as Newcastle strode on to Cochrane Park and the desire shown in the first hit was to dictate the rest of the game.

Liverpool got off the blocks first scoring as Newcastle became over-zealous at the breakdown and gave away a penalty, something which was a real danger with a kicker as deadly as Liverpool's.

Newcastle held their resolve though and rucked like champions to allow an unbelievably destructive Sam Davies to go in under the posts following a break from fly-half Max Nimmo. Gav McMurtry converted.

Again Newcastle allowed their discipline to slip and despite being mere metres into Newcastle's half the Liverpool kicker capitalised. Still Newcastle kept a cool head allowing Nimmo to guide the ball expertly down the field.

The line-out pairing of Greg Bramall and Shaun Stephens took everything that hooker James Buncle could throw at them: this time Stephens collecting the ball for the pack to set up a clinical driving maul taking it all the way for five points.

Liverpool were next to cross the line as one of their two excellent props crashed over to score a converted try.

After the turn around it was a different Newcastle to run out, cutting down on the niggling little mistakes that had stopped the first half flowing quite so well. Prop Chunk Wakefield collected an array of difficult kick-offs and openside Zack King slowed down pretty much every ball to go to ground.

Their hard work paid off as Nimmo read the game like a thirty-year-old to take the ball blind and put a powerful Gav McMurtry into the corner. Nimmo himself converted it.

Next to score was the Liverpool winger who had worked hard for a try all day and had otherwise found his quest fruitless thanks to superb defensive work by Ed Moore and Rob Jackson. It was the destructive Moore and Davies who paired up to batter the ball down the field with Davies again capitalising to put Newcastle eight points clear and take the league.

Captain Stephens was ecstatic with the result, saying: "This is an awesome effort by a team which had been put into a tough league following a re-shuffle of the BUSA programme. The hard work that the guys have put in on the training field and the desire they have for victory is really shown on days like this. It is an absolute pleasure to captain these boys."

Success in the League brought more confrontations with university 1st XVs. Strathclyde University were the next hurdle. *The Courier*'s report of the match:

thecourier

Success all round

NEWCASTLE 2ND XV 28   STRATHCLYDE 1ST XV 17

A different challenge from normal was offered to the Newcastle second string last week, in their first round knock-out in the form of their much older, more generously waisted Scottish opposition.

This was not to say that Newcastle would be bullied about the park, for within minutes the well-drilled Newcastle forwards had beaten Strathclyde at their own game, allowing Alex MacKenzie to score as a result of rolling maul from a line-out. Max Nimmo converted despite strong winds.

Strathclyde's weakness was soon found as Rob Jackson ripped the ball off his opposite number in the Newcastle 22 before skipping and bashing his way more than sixty metres up the park. A resulting scrum allowed No 8 Adam Batson to execute a '8-9-15' move, putting powerful full-back Gav McMurty over in the corner. Again, Nimmo converted.

Strathclyde were eventually allowed to work on their strengths, pushing over a scrum from the five metre line. This was to be the exception, however, as Newcastle's front row, MacKenzie, David 'Fridge' Morgan and David Struth, gritted their teeth and soon got on top of their portly opposition.

With the forwards working hard to create space for the backs, it was never going to be long before centre Ed Moore took his chance (if you can call a halfway line break a chance) to crash over.

Soon more cutting lines from the backs allowed winger Jackson to go between the sticks with a smile on his face, to give Nimmo an easy conversion. Newcastle felt confident enough to make a number of changes at half time.

Seven changes can be expected to rock the boat a little, and it is no surprise that Strathclyde, with their powerful forwards, began to put pressure on the Newcastle line.

The defence though had heart by the bagful, and at times were fighting amongst themselves to make the hit. It was only a late break by the Strathclyde backs that earned them a deserved try. Newcastle were not to be outdone and with fresh resolve, and after a cheeky off-load by lock Shaun Stephens, Ed Moore showed his deadly eye for a finish, once more going over in the corner.

Yet another gutsy and at times polished performance from a tight knit team.

Then, in the quarter-final of the competition, Stirling University 1st XV was beaten 33 – 15.

However, we were about to be brought down to ground, with the most pertinent lesson from the current season, and perhaps a foretaste of the standards to which we must aspire. We suffered a huge defeat to Hartpury College 2nd XV in the semi-final of the Competition. This was one of the best 2nd XVs ever to represent Newcastle University, yet the reverse, 10 – 77, was probably the worst ever defeat suffered by any team in the Club. It was no fluke. Our team did not play particularly badly and were well-beaten by a faster, fitter, more skillful, more committed and much older side.

Third XV

The 3rd XV was in the Northern Conference 3B, together with one 1st XV and two 2nd XVs. It won the league with a 100% record.

Northern Conference 3B League Table 2006/07

	P	W	D	L	Walk-overs	Unplayed	Pts
Newcastle 3rd XV	14	11	0	0	2	1	39
Bradford 1st XV	14	9	1	4	0	0	28
Sheffield Hallam 2nd XV	14	7	0	6	0	1	21
Sheffield 2nd XV	14	7	0	6	0	1	21
Northumbria 3rd XV	14	4	0	8	0	2	12
Leeds Metro. 3rd XV	14	4	0	6	0	4	12
Leeds 3rd XV	14	5	0	7	1	1	12
Sheffield Hallam 3rd XV	14	1	1	11	1	0	1

Our superiority in the company is illustrated by the total annihilation of Bradford's 1st XV, the second placed club, in the final league match of the season. The report in *The Courier*:

thecourier
Newcastle 3rd XV 76
Bradford 1st XV 0

Newcastle's Rugby Thirds opponents Bradford were sitting in second place in the league.

The intensity was high, and the adrenalin pumping. In the first five minutes the forwards smashed the team up the pitch with some quick and aggressive rucking. This set up the backs to run the opposition ragged and produce the first try with a midfield run from Keith Laughlin. Immediately, Bradford's heads dropped and our backs took full advantage skipping through their defence almost at will.

Scores came at regular intervals with the referee abandoning the game with 15 minutes remaining – Bradford's heads were by now down as low as they could go.

The knock-out rounds for the BUSA Vase brought a series of good wins, with an outstanding performance against Aberdeen University 1st XV, away, in the semi-final:

The team that won the 2006/07 BUSA Vase Final. Their coach Mike Doyle is in the 'middle of things'. Photo courtesy of The Courier

First round	Liverpool University 3rd XV	Won	70 – 0
Second round	Sheffield University 3rd XV	Won	17 – 3
Quarter-final	Manchester University 4th XV	Won	22 – 9
Semi-final	Aberdeen University 1st XV	Won	37 – 10

So on to the final and an inspiring display by our team, resulting in an undefeated record for the season. *The Courier* reported:

The Perfect Season

NEWCASTLE UNIVERSITY 3RD XV 38   HARTPURY COLLEGE 3RD XV 12

The perfect end to the perfect season.

Newcastle's Rugby thirds officially swept away all before them this year as they capped off their unbeaten season with a resounding victory over UWE Hartpury in the BUSA vase final.

After 11 wins and no losses in the Northern Conference 3B, the 3rds made their way through to the final and finished off what they duly deserved in emphatic style.

Fly-half Luke Bettesworth truly ran the show, orchestrating a four-try victory, topped off with a near perfect kicking performance. Special mention should also go to centres Mason and his partner Ant Shales who put in some hard hits.

In a match of high standards and impressive rugby, it was somewhat fitting that the man in the middle was the English National referee David Pearson. Pearson will also be the English representative at the Rugby World Cup later this year – a slightly different setting to a sunny day at Cochrane Park.

The standards were set for Newcastle from the outset when outside centre Luke Mason ran in for an early try, the first of a hat-trick, which was duly converted by Bettesworth.

The early score was greeted with great pleasure by the Newcastle supporters who turned out in force for their side's big day, with chants of 'uni' ringing round Cochrane Park, the kind of which are usually reserved for rivals Northumbria.

Mason's second try emerged from a quick release under pressure from Bettesworth who left Mason with a relatively simple short run-in under the posts.

By half-time the score had reached 20 – 7 through two Bettesworth penalties and a conversion, with only a sloppy

234

rolling maul try on the board for the visitors.

The second half was much of the same with an inevitable Newcastle victory always looking the case, despite Hartpury dominating the pack in terms of size. Effort, however, could not be faulted from the smaller Newcastle forwards.

Bettesworth looked the finished article throughout, particularly so when his vision opened up an opportunity for a finely slotted drop goal.

Mason's hat-trick try and a breakaway score from substitute James Gee resulted in a 38 – 12 victory that was much deserved and topped off a truly perfect season.

Luke Bettesworth, stand-off, made a huge contribution with his orchestration of the game and place kicking in the BUSA Vase Final. Photo courtesy of The Courier

'You can't have that, it belongs to us.' Newcastle and Hartpury contest possession in the BUSA Vase Final. Photo courtesy of The Courier

Athletic Union President Anthony Keane presents the BUSA Vase to captain George Fulford-Smith, at the Athletic Union Dinner. Photo courtesy of The Courier

Fourth XV:

The 4th XV were runners-up in the Northern Conference 4B:

Northern Conference 4B League Table 2006/07

	P	W	D	L	Walk-overs	Unplayed	Pts
Sheffield 3rd XV	9	7	0	0	2	0	27
Newcastle 4nd XV	9	5	0	1	3	0	24
Hull 2nd XV	9	4	0	3	2	0	18
York 2nd XV	9	2	0	2	2	3	12
Trinity and All Saints 1st	9	4	0	3	0	2	12
Northumbria 4th XV	9	4	0	3	0	2	12
Huddersfield 1st XV	9	1	0	4	2	2	3
York St John 2nd XV	9	0	1	4	3	1	-2
Leeds Coll. of Music 1st XV	9	0	1	5	3	0	-2
Bradford 2nd XV	9	0	0	2	7	0	-21

The team was then knocked-out, 0 – 43, by Manchester 4th XV in the first round of the BUSA Vase Competition.

19

LESSONS FROM THE PAST.
WHAT OF THE FUTURE?

Rugby football is currently strong at Newcastle. Our senior teams continue to perform well in competition with other leading universities and are undoubtedly respected throughout the BUSA tournaments. While we have always been strong, the all-round standards have probably never been higher than they are now. We can probably claim to be university leaders in promoting the game at all levels. One of our boasts is of the support that we give to the successful Saturday North-east Student League; four of the teams in it are based in the Newcastle University Club and a fifth represents Medicals. Another is in the strength of the inter-mural set-up; it is difficult to imagine that there is a more successful one anywhere in the country. We have also been one of the first universities to spearhead the development of women's rugby, with two XVs now competing in BUSA

The BUSA squad in 2004/05. Photo courtesy of Penguin Photography

competitions. These levels of commitment inevitably result in depth in playing strength and it is noteworthy that our BUSA teams, including the men's 2nd, 3rd, and 4th XV and women's 2nd XV, hold their own against many 1st XV opponents. Similarly, we can field a select side from our intermural teams that gives our men's 1st XV a good run for their money in the annual Director's Challenge.

Nevertheless, we would be very foolish indeed to be complacent in the light of our successes. Our rich history surely teaches us at least one important lesson: we shall have to adapt to whatever changes the future holds for us if we are to remain a significant force in rugby. We cannot live on past, or even present, achievements. We also have to accept that some battles may not be won. We had to withdraw from the national leagues, despite our best efforts to compete in them over four seasons in the late 1980s and early 1990s. One of the sad consequences of our withdrawal from these leagues is that we no longer play and interact with clubs in the region in anything like the way that we did in the past. The University strives to reach out to the rest of the community in sport and other activities and, while it does so successfully in most spheres, there is no doubt that we are much less part of the regional rugby family than was once the case.

So, if we try to gaze into the crystal ball, what is the most serious challenge that lies ahead of us? Perhaps our major problem will be in competing with universities that are prepared to put huge resources into success on the playing field – and may have lower entry standards than those that we demand here. Increasingly, some universities are providing funds for full-time staff appointments to administer and support rugby and are forging close links with professional clubs by sponsoring them. Such moves are unlikely to happen at Newcastle. The University strives for world class standards in teaching, research, scholarship and outreach and, while this provides an outstanding academic environment for any young person, sport must take its place among a range of different activities. However, there are, and probably always will be, outstanding players who seek the security of first class qualifications outside rugby football. Hopefully, they will continue to come to Newcastle where we believe that we can offer the best of all worlds. By developing their potential as rugby players, we will remain in the forefront of the game.

Even so we must keep a watchful eye on outside developments. There are already huge differences in the playing standards of different universities and there are indications that the gaps will go on increasing. The relationships between the academies of the professional clubs and universities are still emerging but they may already be becoming blurred. Hartpury College, which is part of the University of the West of England, has come from literally nowhere to be outstanding in student rugby in recent seasons. This season (2006/07), their 1st and 2nd XVs won, and the 3rd XV were runners-up, in respective BUSA competitions. The explanation is not difficult to find. It can be attributed to a close link with Gloucester Rugby Club Academy, which now has a home at Hartpury! Levels of coaching and other kinds of rugby support are reportedly superb and they certainly set a marker for the aspirations of the rest of us.

One huge asset that we do have, and we must continue to develop and exploit, is that we function as a Club. Newcastle University Rugby Club means so much to generations of players. Our traditions, plus strong committed support from the touchlines, can work wonders for playing results. This was illustrated most recently by the way in which an inspired 3rd XV totally outplayed an excellent Hartpury team because of huge commitment from our players and their support for one another. Realistically however, we cannot ignore the financial demands as the student game becomes increasingly 'professionalised'. We shall have to help ourselves on this front, and this is where everyone associated with the Club can play a significant part. Cumulative 'Pride in the Lion' is surely an excellent focus for players, Vice-Presidents, University alumni, parents and whoever else would like to join us to keep the Club firmly where it belongs – among the very best in student rugby.

'Togetherness'. Playing for one another – the essence of a first-rate Club.
Photo courtesy of Tom McNicholas